America Revised

Also by Frances FitzGerald

Fire in the Lake

Frances FitzGerald

AMERICA REVISED

History Schoolbooks in the Twentieth Century

An Atlantic Monthly Press Book
Little, Brown and Company — Boston — Toronto

FIRST EDITION

LIBRARY OF CONGRESS CATALOGING IN PUBLICATION DATA

FitzGerald, Frances, 1940–
America revised.

"Almost all of the book appeared initially in the New Yorker."
"An Atlantic Monthly Press book."
Bibliography: p.
1. United States—History—Text Books. 2. United States—Historiography. 3. United States—History—Study and teaching. 4. Text-book bias—United States.
I. Title.
E175.85.F57 973'.07'1273 79–16555
ISBN 0–316–28424–6

ATLANTIC–LITTLE, BROWN BOOKS
ARE PUBLISHED BY
LITTLE, BROWN AND COMPANY
IN ASSOCIATION WITH
THE ATLANTIC MONTHLY PRESS

Designed by Susan Windheim

BP

Published simultaneously in Canada
by Little, Brown & Company (Canada) Limited

PRINTED IN THE UNITED STATES OF AMERICA

For my grandmother

Acknowledgments

I am much indebted to friends and colleagues who were kind enough to read this book in manuscript and to give me the benefit of their advice. My particular thanks go to Ronald Steel for his kind encouragement. And to Professor Hazel Hertzberg of Columbia University Teachers College, whose careful criticisms were of enormous importance to me. My readers should not, however, be held responsible for the opinions expressed in the book.

Almost all of the book appeared initially in *The New Yorker*. I am most grateful to Martin Baron, William Shawn, and William Whitworth for all the many improvements they made on the manuscript. Their help was invaluable.

Most of the older history texts I used came from the collection at Columbia University Teachers College. I am most grateful to the librarians there for all of their assistance. My thanks also go to Barbara Grossman and my sister, Joan FitzGerald, without whose enthusiasm and hard labor I could not have completed the book.

America Revised

"The reactions of the textbook business aren't all that fast. It takes five years or more to get a book out, start to finish, so back in the mid-sixties we were really caught. All we had was George Washington Carver in the plates. It was like . . . I remember in the Navy aboard this ship there was a guy who'd call out over the bullhorn every day before mess, 'Time to run the duty chicken into the galley and through the soup.' Well, that's what we did. Ran George Washington Carver through again . . . A bit thin, those books. You can only take so much of peanuts."

In a business not notable for the wit of its personnel, Daniel O'Brian (or so I shall call him) is one of the few people who can adequately describe the atmosphere of the children's textbook industry in the mid- to late sixties when the basso continuo about creeping socialism and evolutionary theory were temporarily overwhelmed by a chorus of protests against the white, male, middle-class orientation of the texts. That period was marked not just by the canonization of George Washington Carver but by the drypointing of white middle-class faces and the hasty appendage of chapters about The Civil Rights Movement or, a year later, The Black Revolution.

"It didn't last too long, that period," O'Brian continued. "Nothing does. I remember the N.C.S.S. (National Council on the Social Studies) Convention in 1968. It was all green. The display rooms were covered with stuff about ecology. The next year there weren't too many green things left. It was all black. Black Studies. And the hardware had all gone — all the audiovisuals vanished. There were only books left and sixteen-millimeter filmstrips with selfthreaders. Now it's drugs. A while ago it was like reading problems — you kept it under the rug. But then the rug hits the ceiling and you're stampeded. Now it's 'Doesn't everyone have a drug problem?' Now that the kids have given it up for alcohol, well, it's all fine, but what about the development costs for these things? Some companies have gone out of business trying to keep up."

Past Masters

THOSE of us who grew up in the fifties believed in the permanence of our American-history textbooks. To us as children, those texts were the truth of things: they were American history. It was not just that we read them before we understood that not everything that is printed is the truth, or the whole truth. It was that they, much more than other books, had the demeanor and trappings of authority. They were weighty volumes. They spoke in measured cadences: imperturbable, humorless, and as distant as Chinese emperors. Our teachers treated them with respect, and we paid them abject homage by memorizing a chapter a week. But now the textbook histories have changed, some of them to such an extent that an adult would find them unrecognizable.

One current junior-high-school American history begins with a story about a Negro cowboy called George McJunkin. It appears that when McJunkin was riding down a lonely trail in New Mexico one cold spring morning in 1925 he discovered a mound containing bones and stone implements, which scientists later proved belonged to an Indian civilization ten thousand years old. The book goes on to say that scientists now believe there were people in the Americas at least twenty thousand years ago. It discusses the Aztec, Mayan, and Incan civilizations and the meaning of the word "culture" before introducing the European explorers.[1]

Another history text — this one for the fifth grade —

begins with the story of how Henry B. Gonzalez, who is a member of Congress from Texas, learned about his own nationality. When he was ten years old, his teacher told him he was an American because he was born in the United States. His grandmother, however, said, "The cat was born in the oven. Does that make him bread?" After reporting that Mr. Gonzalez eventually went to college and law school, the book explains that "the melting pot idea hasn't worked out as some thought it would," and that now "some people say that the people of the United States are more like a salad bowl than a melting pot."[2]

Poor Columbus! He is a minor character now, a walk-on in the middle of American history. Even those books that have not replaced his picture with a Mayan temple or an Iroquois mask do not credit him with discovering America — even for the Europeans. The Vikings, they say, preceded him to the New World, and after that the Europeans, having lost or forgotten their maps, simply neglected to cross the ocean again for five hundred years. Columbus is far from being the only personage to have suffered from time and revision. Captain John Smith, Daniel Boone, and Wild Bill Hickok — the great self-promoters of American history — have all but disappeared, taking with them a good deal of the romance of the American frontier. General Custer has given way to Chief Crazy Horse; General Eisenhower no longer liberates Europe single-handed; and, indeed, most generals, even to Washington and Lee, have faded away, as old soldiers do, giving place to social reformers such as William Lloyd Garrison and Jacob Riis. A number of black Americans have risen to prominence: not only George Washington Carver but Frederick Douglass and Martin Luther King, Jr. W. E. B. Du Bois now invariably accompanies Booker T. Washington. In addition, there is a mystery man called Crispus Attucks, a fugitive slave about whom nothing seems to be known for certain except that he was a victim of the Boston Massacre and thus became one of the first casualties of the American Revolution. Thaddeus Stevens has been reconstructed — his character changed, as it were, from black to white, from cruel and vindictive to persistent and sincere. As for Teddy Roosevelt, he now champions the issue of conservation instead of charging up San Juan Hill. No single President really stands out as a hero, but all Presidents — except certain unmentionables in the second half of the nineteenth century — seem to have done as well as could be expected, given difficult circumstances.

Of course, when one thinks about it, it is hardly surprising that modern scholarship and modern perspectives have found their way into children's books. Yet the changes remain shocking. Those who in the sixties complained of the bland optimism, the chauvinism, and the materialism of their old civics texts did so in the belief that, for all their protests, the texts would never change. The thought must have had something reassuring about it, for that generation never noticed when its complaints began to take effect and the songs about radioactive rainfall and houses made of ticky-tacky began to appear in the textbooks. But this is what happened.

The history texts now hint at a certain level of unpleasantness in American history. Several books, for instance, tell the story of Ishi, the last "wild" Indian in the continental United States, who, captured in 1911 after the massacre of his tribe, spent the final four and a half years of his life in the University of California's museum of anthropology, in San Francisco. At least three books show the same stunning picture of the breaker boys, the child coal miners of Pennsylvania — ancient children with deformed bodies and blackened faces who stare stupidly out from the entrance to a mine. One book quotes a soldier on the use of torture in the American campaign to pacify the Philippines at the beginning of the century. A number of books say that during the American Revolution the patriots tarred and feathered those who did not support them, and drove many of the loyalists from the country. Almost all the present-day history books note that the United States interned Japanese-Americans in detention camps during the Second World War.

Ideologically speaking, the histories of the fifties were implacable, seamless. Inside their covers, America was perfect: the greatest nation in the world, and the embodiment of democracy, freedom, and technological progress. For them, the country never changed in any important way: its values and its political institutions remained constant from the time of the American Revolution. To my generation — the children of the fifties — these texts appeared permanent just because they were so self-contained. Their orthodoxy, it seemed, left no handholds for attack, no lodging for decay. Who, after all, would dispute the wonders of technology or the superiority of the English colonists over the Spanish? Who would find fault with the pastorale of the West or the Old South? Who would question the anti-Communist crusade? There was, it seemed, no point in comparing these visions with reality, since they were the public truth and were thus quite irrelevant to what existed and to what anyone privately believed. They were — or so it seemed — the permanent expression of mass culture in America.

But now the texts have changed, and with them the country that American children are growing up into. The society that was once uniform is now a patchwork of rich and poor, old and young, men and women, blacks, whites, Hispanics, and Indians. The system that ran so smoothly by means of the Constitution under the guidance of benevolent conductor Presidents is now a rattletrap affair. The past is no highway to the present; it is a collection of issues and events that do not fit together and that lead in no single direction. The word "progress" has been replaced by the word "change": children, the modern texts insist, should learn history so that they can adapt to the rapid changes taking place around them. History is proceeding in spite of us. The present, which was once portrayed in the concluding chapters as a peaceful haven of scientific advances and Presidential inaugurations, is now a tangle of problems: race problems, urban problems, foreign-policy problems, problems of pollution, poverty, energy depletion, youthful rebellion, assassination, and drugs. Some books illustrate these problems dramatically. One, for instance, contains a picture of a doll half buried in a mass of untreated sewage; the caption reads, "Are we in danger of being overwhelmed by the products of our society and wastage created by their production? Would you agree with this photographer's interpretation?"[3] Two books show the same picture of an old black woman sitting in a straight chair in a dingy room, her hands folded in graceful resignation;[4] the surrounding text discusses the problems faced by the urban poor and by the aged who depend on Social Security. Other books present current problems less starkly. One of the texts concludes sagely:

Problems are part of life. Nations face them, just as people face them, and try to solve them. And today's Americans have one great advantage over past generations. Never before have

Americans been so well equipped to solve their problems. They have today the means to conquer poverty, disease, and ignorance. The technetronic age has put that power into their hands.[5]

Such passages have a familiar ring. Amid all the problems, the deus ex machina of science still dodders around in the gloaming of pious hope.

Even more surprising than the emergence of problems is the discovery that the great unity of the texts has broken. Whereas in the fifties all texts represented the same political view, current texts follow no pattern of orthodoxy. Some books, for instance, portray civil-rights legislation as a series of actions taken by a wise, paternal government; others convey some suggestion of the social upheaval involved and make mention of such people as Stokely Carmichael and Malcolm X. In some books, the Cold War has ended; in others, it continues, with Communism threatening the free nations of the earth.

The political diversity in the books is matched by a diversity of pedagogical approach. In addition to the traditional narrative histories, with their endless streams of facts, there are so-called "discovery," or "inquiry," texts, which deal with a limited number of specific issues in American history. These texts do not pretend to cover the past; they focus on particular topics, such as "stratification in Colonial society" or "slavery and the American Revolution," and illustrate them with documents from primary and secondary sources. The chapters in these books amount to something like case studies, in that they include testimony from people with different perspectives or conflicting views on a single subject. In addition, the chapters provide background information, explanatory notes, and a series of questions for the student. The questions are the heart of the matter, for when they are carefully selected they force students to think much as historians think: to define the point of view of the speaker, analyze the ideas presented, question the relationship between events, and so on. One text, for example, quotes Washington, Jefferson, and John Adams on the question of foreign alliances and then asks, "What did John Adams assume that the international situation would be after the American Revolution? What did Washington's attitude toward the French alliance seem to be? How do you account for his attitude?" Finally, it asks, "Should a nation adopt a policy toward alliances and cling to it consistently, or should it vary its policies toward other countries as circumstances change?"[6] In these books, history is clearly not a list of agreed-upon facts or a sermon on politics but a babble of voices and a welter of events which must be ordered by the historian.

In matters of pedagogy, as in matters of politics, there are not two sharply differentiated categories of books; rather, there is a spectrum. Politically, the books run from moderate left to moderate right; pedagogically, they run from the traditional history sermons, through a middle ground of narrative texts with inquiry-style questions and of inquiry texts with long stretches of narrative, to the most rigorous of case-study books. What is common to the current texts — and makes all of them different from those of the fifties — is their engagement with the social sciences. In eighth-grade histories, the "concepts" of social science make fleeting appearances. But these "concepts" are the very foundation stones of various elementary-school social-studies series. The 1970 Harcourt Brace Jovanovich series, for example, boasts in its preface of "a horizontal base or ordering of conceptual schemes" to match its "vertical arm of behavioral themes."[7] What this means is not entirely clear, but the books do proceed from easy questions to hard ones, such as — in the sixth-grade book — "How was interaction between merchants and citizens different in the Athenian and Spartan social systems?" Virtually all the American-history texts for older children include discussions of "role," "status," and "culture." Some of them stage debates between eminent social scientists in roped-off sections of the text; some include essays on economics or sociology; some contain pictures and short biographies of social scientists of both sexes and of diverse races. Many books seem to accord social scientists a higher status than American Presidents.

Quite as striking as these political and pedagogical alterations is the change in the physical appearance of the texts. The schoolbooks of the fifties showed some effort in the matter of design: they had maps, charts, cartoons, photographs, and an occasional four-color picture to break up the columns of print. But beside the current texts they look as naïve as Soviet fashion magazines. The print in the fifties books is heavy and far too black, the colors muddy. The photographs are conventional news shots — portraits of Presidents in three-quarters profile, posed "action" shots of soldiers. The other illustrations tend to be Socialist-realist-style drawings (there are a lot of hefty farmers with hoes in the Colonial-period chapters) or incredibly vulgar made-for-children paintings of patriotic events. One painting shows Columbus standing in full court dress on a beach in the New World from a perspective that could have belonged only to the Arawaks. By contrast, the current texts are paragons of sophisticated modern design. They look not like *People* or *Family Circle* but, rather, like *Architectural Digest* or *Vogue*. One of them has an Abstract Expressionist design on its cover, another a Rauschenberg-style collage, a third a reproduction of an American primitive painting. Inside, almost all of them have a full-page reproduction of a painting of the New York school — a Jasper Johns flag, say, or "The Boston Massacre," by Larry Rivers. But these reproductions are separated only with difficulty from the over-all design, for the time charts in the books look like Noland stripe paintings, and the distribution charts are as punctilious as Albers' squares in their color gradings. The amount of space given to illustrations is far greater than it was in the fifties; in fact, in certain "slow-learner" books the pictures far outweigh the text in importance. However, the illustrations have a much greater historical value. Instead of made-up paintings or anachronistic sketches, there are cartoons, photographs, and paintings drawn from the periods being treated. The chapters on the Colonial period will show, for instance, a ship's carved prow, a Revere bowl, a Copley painting — a whole gallery of Early Americana. The nineteenth century is illustrated with nineteenth-century cartoons and photographs — and the photographs are all of high artistic quality. As for the twentieth-century chapters, they are adorned with the contents of a modern-art museum.

The use of all this art and high-quality design contains some irony. The nineteenth-century photographs of child laborers or urban slum apartments are so beautiful that they transcend their subjects. To look at them, or at the Victor Gatto painting of the Triangle shirtwaist-factory fire, is to see not misery or ugliness but an art object. In the modern chapters, the contrast between style and content is just as great: the color photographs of junkyards or polluted rivers look as enticing as *Gourmet*'s photographs of food. The book that is perhaps the most stark in its description of modern problems illustrates the horrors of nuclear testing with a pretty Ben Shahn picture of the Bikini explosion, and the potential for global ecological disaster with a color photograph of the planet swirling its mantle of white clouds.[8] Whereas in the nineteen-fifties the texts were childish in the sense that they were naïve and clumsy, they are now childish in the sense that they are polymorphous-perverse. American history is not dull any longer; it is a sensuous experience.

The surprise that adults feel in seeing the changes in history texts must come from the lingering hope that there is, somewhere out there, an objective truth. The hope is, of course, foolish. All of us children of the twentieth century know, or should know, that there are no absolutes in human affairs, and thus there can be no such thing as perfect objectivity. We know that each historian in some degree creates the world anew and that all history is in some degree contemporary history. But beyond this knowledge there is still a hope for some reliable authority, for some fixed stars in the universe. We may know journalists cannot be wholly unbiased and that "balance" is an imaginary point between two extremes, and yet we hope that Walter Cronkite will tell us the truth of things. In the same way, we hope that our history will not change — that we learned the truth of things as children. The texts, with their impersonal voices, encourage this hope, and therefore it is particularly disturbing to see how they change, and how fast.

Slippery history! Not every generation but every few years the content of American-history books for children changes appreciably. Schoolbooks are not, like trade books, written and left to their fate. To stay in step with the cycles of "adoption" in school districts across the country, the publishers revise most of their old texts or substitute new ones every three or four years. In the process of revision, they not only bring history up to date but make changes — often substantial changes — in the body of the work. History books for children are thus more contemporary than any other form of history. How should it be otherwise? Should students read histories written ten, fifteen, thirty years ago? In theory, the system is reasonable — except that each generation of children reads only one generation of schoolbooks. That transient history is those children's history forever — their particular version of America.

The nature of the influence that these textbooks have on children is, of course, another matter. Many studies have been done on the question of what seventeen- or eighteen-year-old Americans know about their history and their political system, with uniformly depressing results. A recent survey by the National Assessment of Educational Progress showed that forty-seven per cent of the nation's seventeen-year-olds did not know that each state has two United States senators.[9] A wholly unscientific survey of my own would show that few American adults can remember as much as the name of the history textbook they "had" in secondary school. And the sight of an old textbook is much less likely to bring back the sequence of Presidents or the significance of the Hawley-Smoot Tariff Act than it is to evoke the scene of an eighth-grade classroom: the sight of, say, Peggy, one long leg wrapped around the other, leaning forward on the scarred green bench, or Stevie talking a mile a minute and excitedly twirling his persistent cowlick. Rabbits, it is said, cannot remember pain or fear for more than sixty seconds. Perhaps human beings cannot remember things that bored them. Memory has its own antidotes. On the other hand, the fact that one cannot remember the order of the Presidents does not mean that all is lost. Amid the telephone numbers, nursery rhymes, and advertising jingles that we carry around in our heads, there are often snatches of textbook history. My own snatches consist of visual images detached from their context: Balboa on his peak in Darien; the supporters of Andrew Jackson celebrating his first election by tromping over the White House furniture in their muddy boots. Other people have more literary memories. "I had Muzzey," one friend told me recently. "Wonderful book. I'll never forget the scene of Lincoln after the Battle of Gettysburg looking over the graves in the cemetery and a voice crying out to him, 'Calhooon! Calhoooon!' " The memory of my friend was not, as it turned out, perfectly accurate, for in David Saville Muzzey's *American History* William Lloyd Garrison is speaking at a banquet in Charleston after the war, and about him Muzzey asks rhetorically, "Did the echoes of his voice reach a grave over which stood a marble stone engraved with the single word 'Calhoun'?"[10] Still, my friend had remembered the dramatic irony, and that was surely the essence of this particular passage.

In some general sense, this may be the truth of the matter: what sticks to the memory from those textbooks is not any particular series of facts but an atmosphere, an impression, a tone. And this impression may be all the more influential just because one cannot remember the facts and arguments that created it. In the fifties, we learned from our texts — math and English as well as history — that Americans were a tolerant people, full of common sense, practical, industrious, democratic, civic-minded, and generally homogeneous. That we, then or later, read about Cotton Mather, slavery and the Civil War, Thoreau, the

Molly Maguires, and vigilante rule in San Francisco somehow did not cause us to alter this impression. It was only the events of the nineteen-sixties that changed it. To learn that Americans were also violent, idealistic, and divided by race and culture was not just to learn something new but to undergo a reëducation. What the current texts say about the American Revolution or the Vietnam War may therefore have some importance: though the memory of children may reduce much of it to white sound, some may remain as a tone of voice, a definition of the register.

In the nineteenth century, a heavy reliance on textbooks was the distinguishing mark of American education; it was called "the American system" by Europeans. The texts were substitutes for well-trained teachers; in some parts of the country, they constituted the whole of a school's library and the only books a child would ever read on the subject of, say, American history. Now, of course, the texts must compete not only with other books but with magazines, movies, television, and so on. The problem for the modern child is not so much to acquire information as to select from the barrage of it coming from everywhere, including the corner of the living room. As part of an attempt to develop such powers of discrimination, many teachers now use the texts critically, as they would any other book.*

* Not as many, however, as one might think. In 1976 the National Science Foundation commissioned three studies of the status of science, mathematics and social-studies education in the United States. On the basis of these studies the president of the National Council on the Social Studies and two other professors of education concluded that a) The dominant instructional tool continues to be the conventional textbook, and longtime best-sellers continue to dominate the market and b) Teachers tend not only to rely on, but to believe in, the textbook as the source of knowledge. Textbooks are not seen as support materials, but as the central instrument of instruction by most social-studies teachers. Shaver, James P., O. L. Davis, Jr. and Suzanne W. Helburn. "The Status of Social Studies Education: Impressions from Three NSF Studies." *Social Education*. Feb., 1979, pp. 150–153.

(One teacher in a rural Maine school says that he uses a conservative, ten-year-old history text, because its views and his own views differ so strongly.) The texts still give a structure to history courses — and they are still the only books that many children ever read on the subject — but they have lost their single voice of authority. Yet, no matter what degree of influence the texts actually have on children, they have their own intrinsic interest as historical documents. For they are not, like other books, works of single authors. Many people have a hand in writing them, and they are tailored to please a public that extends even beyond the vast educational establishment. Consensus documents, they are themselves a part of history, in that they reflect the concerns, the conventional wisdom, and even the fads of the age that produced them.

Charles and Mary Beard, Richard Hofstadter, Merle Curti, John Hope Franklin, Ernest R. May, Henry Steele Commager, Henry F. Graff — the names of some of the most distinguished American historians appear on the covers of high-school textbooks of American history. Their names usually appear as part of duos or trios: Graff and Krout; Todd and Curti; Caughey, Franklin, and May; Barker, Dodd, and Commager. Some of the high-school books — and most of the eighth-grade books — also bear the name of a professor of education, a high-school teacher, or a school administrator. But there is almost always the name of an academic historian with impressive credentials. What these names signify is, however, questionable.

Children cannot be expected to care very much who wrote their texts. But any history teacher glancing through the popular texts of past and present must wonder a good deal about the relationship of these famous men to their works. The texts do not usually say it, but any biographical dictionary will show that a number of the distinguished historians named on the covers died long before the current editions of the texts were published. Sad though this may be, what is interesting is that they died before the occurrence of many of the events they are credited with describing. A teacher who looked through a number of texts would discover that since the nineteen-thirties all historians have written their textbooks in much the same style — indeed, in a style that can only be described as textbook prose. Reading a few paragraphs here and there, the teacher would almost certainly be struck by certain discrepancies — certain ideas quite foreign to the authors. For instance, Richard Hofstadter's *A People and a Nation* (Clarence L. Ver Steeg, co-author) contains the thought that the immigrants of the late nineteenth century "introduced variety into American life, adding immeasurably to its color and interest," and that "in time they showed their ability to enter the mainstream of American life without giving up either their identity or their distinctive qualities."[11] It's hard to believe Hofstadter, that brilliant stylist and caustic critic of American liberalism, could have written such a sentence. Similarly, many of the texts omit or contradict the very interpretations of history which their supposed authors made famous: Charles and Mary Beard's school history scants economics as a factor in the making of the Constitution; the nineteen-thirties text that bears Commager's name contains no intellectual history at all. Finally, the difference between two editions of the same text is often so great that a historian would have had to undergo a conversion, or possession by another historian, in order to write both.

The internal evidence of a text is enough to show that

the relationship to it of the historian whose name appears on its title page is rarely the simple one of author. But any teacher who wanted to find out just what that relationship is would run into difficulties. In the first place, there is a great deal of secrecy in the textbook business. Not just the publishers and editors but the authors as well do not care to explain exactly how texts come into being. And teachers permit them to maintain this silence. In the second place, the making of a text is a complicated business — much more complicated than the making of a trade book. Texts are not "written" anymore; they are, as the people in the industry say, "developed," and this process involves large numbers of people and many compromises. Not since the twenties have textbook publishers commissioned a basic history text from a single author and simply printed it, as they would a trade book. The costs are too great, the risks too high, and the demands from the schools too exacting. Typically, the first step in the current process is to find two or more authorities in the field, including one academic historian and one schoolteacher or administrator. (The exceptions are in the preparation of non-mass-market books for very literate high-school students.) The rationale is that a specialist in history and a specialist in children can write a better text together than either could alone. But — like most educational theories — this assumption cannot be proved or disproved, since the text houses often choose both specialists for their prestige or their influence with school boards rather than for their skill in collaborating on the writing of histories for children. As a rule, the younger the audience the book is intended for, the greater the number of specialists involved. The high-school books usually have two authors' names on the cover; the eighth-grade books usually have three; and the social-studies series running from kindergarten through the sixth grade have a whole raft of them. A new Houghton Mifflin social-studies series, for instance, has two authors, a general editor, an editorial adviser, and nine consultants, including a consultant for "skills" and one for "values." What all these people actually do on the books is not entirely clear, but their names give the series a certain weight of authority.

Whether a publisher has chosen his authors well or badly, his editors usually have a fairly exact idea of what should go into the book he has commissioned. In the first place, they have read the texts for college students, and these show what is necessary in the way of scholarly furnishings. In the second place, they have analyzed the competition, so they know what is selling in the school systems. At one publishing company I visited, the social-studies editor was doing a line count of the ten best-selling eighth-grade histories to find out how much space each gave to each major event in American history. At another company, an editor was writing a perceptive analysis of the changes in the content of history books over the past five years. In doing such studies, text editors may be trying to duplicate the most popular features of the competition in one book or they may be trying to find a hole in the market for a new kind of book. If it is the latter, the editors will also be guided by their other sources of information about the market — ranging from educational-research surveys, through pilot studies of new materials, to the reports of their salesmen. Whatever their goal may be, they usually start by giving the authors an outline to follow.

In the matter of prose style, the editors invariably impose constraints on the writer. The public schools require that all textbooks be adjusted to the standard reading levels for the grades that the books are intended for. The text houses must therefore see to it that all manuscripts follow standard "readability" formulas, which measure the frequency with which difficult words occur and the complexity of the sentence structure. The Dale-Chall formula, for example, gives a list of three thousand "easy" words (the list includes "banjo," "bobwhite," and "beautify" but not "special," "necessary," or "disease") and a complicated equation between the number of difficult words and the length of sentences. Since few historians can contrive to write by these rules, the editors usually have to rewrite the final draft. In the process, they may or may not change the essential meaning of the original, but, almost necessarily, they remove all individuality from the writing, homogenizing it so that it is in fact nearly unreadable.

In respect to political content, too, the editors have a fairly good idea of what will and what will not sell. A few years ago, for example, the editors at one house were giving their writers specific instructions to highlight ecology and minority groups. A history book, they said, would not sell in Texas if it did not have a good deal of material on Mexican-Americans, and it would not sell anywhere if it had pictures of minority-group members who were not *aspiring* people: pictures of black sharecroppers could not be used in order to illustrate Reconstruction; if blacks were pictured they had to be, say, technicians in lab coats. Some of the political criteria change from year to year, but at any given moment most text editors have the same kind of information and thus tend to think alike on most subjects. To look through all the junior-high-school textbooks published in 1975 and 1976 is to see that all use virtually the same formulas to describe both the Vietnam War and Watergate. The editors give much more political as well as stylistic latitude to authors of texts for literate eleventh or twelfth graders than to authors of histories for the lower grades, with the result that only the very sophisticated texts contain any original historical writing.

The text editors are not, of course, always right in their judgments about content. They have their problems, too. In certain periods, such as the sixties, educational and political styles change faster than texts can be written and marketed. Since present-day texts are expected to cover everything up to the moment, events are bound to outpace them. The assassination of President Kennedy and Watergate created special consternation in houses that had issued their histories just before the events occurred, for these houses were stuck for a time with sanguine last chapters on the achievements of the Kennedy or the Nixon Administration. A perpetual problem for the editors is that Presidential elections come every four years. In one case, when a book was to be published just after an election the editors asked the authors to write two versions of the concluding pages, one describing victory for the incumbent, the other defeat; both versions, of course, had to fit in with the seamless web of American history. The editors thought they would be able to choose between the two at the last moment. But both versions described John F. Kennedy as the incumbent candidate in 1964.

The publishing houses do occasionally print manuscripts more or less as they arrive — some authors write very well to the editorial requirements — but usually the editing is heavy. When it happens that the editors want an author's name more than his work, they may take a manuscript that is utterly inadequate to their purposes and rewrite the whole thing. One young woman I met had in the two years of her employment at Holt, Rinehart & Winston, in the sixties, rewritten part of one of the best-known of the inquiry texts and written from scratch part of the teacher's guide for another history text. She had also, and with little help, written a book of short biographies of famous Americans which her house published under the name of an elementary-school teacher. The young editor had no academic credentials in history or education and no teaching experience; her annual salary for those incredibly productive years was six thousand dollars — a small fraction of what a distinguished figurehead receives for not writing a book.

Recently, a few publishing companies in the social-science field have taken the logical next step and eliminated these highly paid non-authors entirely, putting out so-called "managed texts," which list no author but merely an editor whose name carries prestige. The editor writes an introduction or one chapter of the book (or has it written for him) and farms out the rest to graduate students, free-lance writers, and other cheap intellectual labor. Since these laborers — if they are responsible — must rehash the work of experts in the field, the managed texts often flirt with the laws on plagiarism. Still, in some respects their truth-in-packaging is greater than that of many texts whose covers claim authorship by well-known scholars.

Not even a book in print is safe from editorial intervention, for if it is successful it will be revised and reissued every three or four years, in time to be presented anew to the school systems. The revisions can be small or extensive, but even the small ones can be fairly drastic in political terms. In the mid-seventies, two high-school histories by different authors which were published by Holt, Rinehart & Winston appeared with their discussions of the Cold War altered completely — from a Cold Warrior to a revisionist position.[12] A book that survives for ten years will receive a complete overhaul and a historical update. If you look through the various editions of the very long-lived texts, you will see the book changing like a Brunswick stew or a customized stock car. After thirty years or so, the latest edition will show very little trace of the original. One of the most popular eighth-grade histories, a book known as Casner and Gabriel, began in the thirties as a liberal internationalist book and by the fifties had changed into a fierce anti-Communist tract.

To the uninitiated, the very thought of what goes on in a textbook house must inspire a good deal of vertigo. Way up in some office building sit people — ordinary mortals with red and blue pencils — deciding all the issues of American history, not to mention those of literature and biology. What shall we think of the Vietnam War? Of the American Revolution? What is the nature of American society and what are its values? The responsibility of these people seems awesome, for, as is not true of trade publishers, the audiences for their products are huge, impressionable, and captive. Children have to read textbooks; they usually have to read all of each textbook and are rarely asked to criticize it for style or point of view. A textbook is there, much like Mt. Everest awaiting George Mallory, and it leaves no alternative. The textbook editors, therefore, must appear to be the arbiters of American values, and the publishing companies the Ministries of Truth for children. With such power over the past and the future, textbook people — or so the uninitiated assume — should all be philosophers. Oddly, however, few people in the textbook business seem to reflect on their role as truth givers. And most of them are reluctant to discuss the content of their books. Occasionally, a young editor full of injured idealism will "leak" a piece of information about house policy. In one publishing house, a young woman pulled me inside her office conspiratorially to show me a newspaper article attacking a literary anthology that her company had published a few years before. The article expressed outrage about the profanity in the book, pointing to the use of the word "damn" in one short story. "Don't tell anyone I showed you this, or I'll lose my job," the young woman whispered. She went on to say that she had had to revise the anthology — a task that consisted of removing the offending selection and finding stories by two American women and a Puerto Rican man to replace three short stories by Anglo-Saxon men.

"Isn't that a bit arbitrary?" I asked.

"Oh, yes," she said. "But, you see, we're under such great pressure. We'd never sell the book without a Hispanic-American."

The reticence of the textbook people derives, one soon discovers, from the essential ambiguity of their position. On one hand, they are running what amount to Ministries of Truth for children, and, on the other, they are simply trying to make money in one of the freest of free enterprises in the United States, where companies often go under. The market sets limits to the publishers' truth-giving powers. These limits are invisible to outsiders, and they shift like sandbars over time, but the textbook people have a fairly good sense of where they are likely to run aground — and for the rest they feel their way along. Under the circumstances, there is no point in discussing final, or even intermediate, principles, since these would merely upset the navigation. It takes someone used to operating under the norms of trade publishing to demonstrate where principles conflict with market realities.

Robert Bernstein, the president of Random House, runs a large book-publishing complex. In 1974, the head of Pantheon, a Random House division, showed Bernstein the manuscript of what Bernstein thought was an excellent new ninth-grade history of Mississippi. The product of a collaboration between students and faculty of Tougaloo and Millsaps Colleges, the book, unlike the old textbook in use in Mississippi schools, discussed racial conflict frankly and pointed out the contributions that black people had made to the state. The manuscript had been turned down by several textbook houses, but Bernstein — against the advice of some of his own textbook people — backed its publication as a textbook. Pantheon published it as both a trade book and a textbook, under the title *Mississippi: Conflict and Change.* Most of the books never left the warehouse, because the one customer for them, the Mississippi State Textbook Purchasing Board, refused to approve the text for use in state schools at state expense, even though the one textbook in use had gone largely unchanged for ten years and the board was authorized to approve as many as five state histories. As an activist in civil-rights and civil-liberties causes, Bernstein was outraged. So were the authors of the book, and so were some parents, students, and local school officials in Mississippi, and they retained the N.A.A.C.P. Legal Defense and Educational Fund to file suit against the Mississippi State Textbook Purchasing Board on the ground that its one approved history deprecated black Mississippians and championed white supremacy. "This business is shockingly political," Bernstein told me. "Especially in the South it's shocking."

Shocking as it might be, though, Random House did not join the Legal Defense Fund in bringing suit. Historically, textbook houses do not bring such actions, and rarely, if ever, do they protest when their books are banned by school authorities or burned by outraged citizens. Unlike many trade publishers in similar circumstances (and unlike Pantheon in this case), they acquiesce, give way to pressure, and often cut out the offending passages. In the fall of 1974, a group of parents and other citizens in Kanawha County, West Virginia, demonstrated and finally shut down schools throughout the county in protest against some books newly acquired for classroom use or for the school libraries. Among the objects of their wrath were a number of stories by black writers (the protesters claimed that these were critical of whites), an anti-war poem, and a Mark Twain satire on the Book of Genesis. The incident made national news for weeks and created a good deal of consternation among publishers, teachers, and civil-liberties groups. The Teacher Rights Division of the National Education Association studied the controversy and concluded, not surprisingly, that it was basically a cultural conflict between liberal values and the fundamentalists beliefs of the community.[13] No national organization found anything objectionable in the books, and yet at least one publishing house revised its literary anthology to meet Kanawha County standards.

Trade-book publishers tend to look upon such incidents as First Amendment issues, and to see the acquiescence of textbook publishers as pure cowardice—as a betrayal of civil-liberties principles for commercial ends. But there is a sense in which they are wrong. For it is one thing to defend the right to publish a book and quite another to insist that schools must use the book. Why should the editors of Random House, Rand McNally, or Ginn & Company act as the arbiters of the classroom? Who are they to insist that children read Langston Hughes instead of

Henry Wadsworth Longfellow, or works by three Anglo-Saxon men instead of works by two American women and one Hispanic-American man? A group like the National Education Association or the Legal Defense Fund can bring a case against a school board for censorship. But textbook publishers are only the servants of the schools, the providers of what they require. And yet textbook publishers rarely make this argument, since, taken to its logical conclusion, it implies that they have — and should have — no standards; that truth is a market commodity, determined by what will sell. Naturally, the publishers do not want to make this admission; hence the swampiness of their public statements, and their strangely unfocussed anxiety when they're asked about their editorial decisions.

To look further into the question of textbook selection and rejection is to see that there is some matter of principle involved. In most countries, national authorities — academies or Ministries of Education — more or less dictate educational policy and the content of textbooks. But the American educational system has always been highly decentralized, and resistant to national authority of any sort. From the publishers' point of view, the educational system is a market, but from the point of view of the schools it is a rough kind of democracy. If a state or a school district wants a certain kind of textbook — a certain kind of truth — should it not have it? The truth is everywhere political, and this system is in principle no less reasonable and no more oppressive of the individual than the alternative of a national authority. In fact, it might be argued that it is less oppressive — that, given the size of the United States, the texts reflect the values and attitudes of society at large much more accurately than they would without decentralization. At least to some degree, they reflect the society itself.

The texts represent the society imperfectly, because the democracy of the educational system is not perfect. In the first place, texts are chosen by adults, and not by the children who must read them. An alternative system is difficult to conceive, but the fact remains that the texts do not represent children. In the second place, not all adults, or even all teachers, have a voice in the selection of schoolbooks. The system of selection is far from uniform across the country, and depends upon a variety of institutions analogous to the Electoral College or to the Senate as it was conceived by the Founding Fathers. About half of the states, for instance, have some form of state-level control over the selection of elementary-school textbooks; slightly fewer states have that control over the choice of secondary-school textbooks. In most of these states, a board of education, a superintendent of schools, or a special textbook committee reviews all texts submitted by the publishers and lists or adopts a certain number of them in each category for use in the public schools. The practices of these review boards vary widely, as does their membership. Some boards, for instance, can by law adopt only a few books in each category, and in practice they may, as the one in Mississippi did, adopt only one. Others simply weed out a few books they judge substandard and leave the real power of decision to the schools. In the so-called non-adoption states, the school districts usually have committees to examine the texts, and the practices of the committees differ more than those of the state boards. The system is, in fact, so complicated nationwide that publishers employ people to spend most of their time figuring out how it works.

The theory behind the practice of state- or districtwide adoptions is that some educational authority should stand between the world of commerce and the hard-pressed teachers to insure that the books meet certain educational standards. The standards are not, however, entirely academic. The guidelines for most state boards include dicta on the subject matter of the books and on the attitudes they display. The 1976 guidelines of the State Instructional Materials Councils for Florida, for instance, note, "Instructional materials should accurately portray man's place in ecological systems, including the necessity for the protection of our environment and conservation of our natural resources. [They] should encourage thrift and humane treatment of people and should not contain any material reflecting unfairly upon persons because of their race, color, creed, national origin, ancestry, sex, or occupation."[14] The State of Oregon has traditionally prohibited its schools from using texts that speak slightingly of the Founding Fathers. In some cases, the unwritten criteria of state boards are more specific and more important to the selection of books; in certain instances, they contradict the written guidelines.

Then, too, the whole system is less than democratic, because it is biassed toward the large adoption units — the large adoption states and the big-city school districts — and particularly biassed toward the ones that make a narrow selection of books. For example, the recommendation of a social-studies book by the Texas State Textbook Committee can make a difference of hundreds of thousands of dollars to a publisher. Consequently, that committee has traditionally had a strong influence on the content of texts. In certain periods, the committee has made it worthwhile for publishers to print a special Lone Star edition of American history, for use in Texas alone. Much more important, it has from time to time exercised veto power over the content of texts used nationwide. For example, in 1961 a right-wing fringe group called Texans for America intimidated the committee, and it pressed several publishers to make substantial changes in their American-history and geography texts. Macmillan, for one, deleted a passage saying that the Second World War might have been averted if the United States had joined the League of Nations. The Silver Burdett Company took out two passages concerning the need for the United States to maintain friendly relations with other countries and the possibility that some countries would occasionally disagree with us and substituted passages saying that some countries were less free than the United States. Various publishers deleted references to Pete Seeger, Langston Hughes, and several other offenders against the sensibilities of Texans for America.[15] Not only the largest states but combinations of smaller ones have often exerted an influence disproportionate to the size of their school populations. The fact that most of the former Confederate states have state-level adoptions has meant that until recently conservative white school boards have imposed their racial prejudices not only on the children in their states but on children throughout the nation.

In sum, the system of adoptions has a significant impact on the way Americans are taught their own history. Because of the Texas State Textbook Committee, New England children, whose ancestors heartily disapproved of the Mexican War, have grown up with heroic tales of Davy Crockett and Sam Houston. Because of actions taken by the Detroit school board and the Newark Textbook

Council in the early sixties, textbooks began for the first time to treat the United States as a multiracial society.

The school establishment is not the only group that shapes American history in the textbooks. It is often private-interest groups or citizens' organizations that bring about the most important political changes in the texts. The voices of these outside pressure groups have risen and fallen almost rhythmically in the course of the past fifty years. Sometimes there seems to be a great deal of public interest in textbooks, sometimes very little. What is noteworthy is that until 1960 the voices were pretty much alike; after that, they became much more varied, and the public debate over texts altered dramatically.

The history of public protests against textbooks goes back at least to the middle of the nineteenth century, but these protests grew in size and intensity with the establishment of universal secondary education, in the twentieth. The first important outbreak of them occurred in the years following the First World War. In that period, the mayor of Chicago and the Hearst newspapers, using adjectives such as "unpatriotic" and "un-American," created an uproar over what they said was the pro-British bias of certain texts. (According to Henry Steele Commager, one of the objects of their rage was an account of the battle of Bunker Hill in a text by Andrew C. McLaughlin. That being a simpler era in the history of textbook publishing, McLaughlin himself answered the charges. According to Commager, he volunteered to change a sentence that read, "Three times the British returned courageously to the attack" to one reading, "Three times the cowardly British returned to the attack.") Simultaneously, the Daughters of the American Revolution attacked some of the texts for not putting enough stress on American military history. The Ku Klux Klan got into the act by complaining of pro-Jewish and pro-Catholic sentiments. Then a number of fundamentalist groups protested against the teaching of evolutionary theory, and eventually succeeded in purging some biology texts of references to evolution. Finally, and with no publicity at all, several utilities associations, including the National Electric Light Association, the American Gas Association, and the American Railway Association, put pressure on the publishers and school officials to doctor the texts in their favor. They got results until their efforts were discovered by the Federal Trade Commission.[16] This wave of right-wing indignation receded as the Depression hit, and for the next ten years such groups remained silent. During the thirties, the peace was broken only by the Women's Christian Temperance Union and the liquor interests, whose debate seems to have ended in a draw.

Then, in 1939, there erupted the most furious of all textbook controversies to date, the subject of which was a series on American civilization by Dr. Harold Rugg. A professor at Columbia University Teachers College, Dr. Rugg had written his series (intended for pupils in elementary and junior high school) in the twenties and had begun publishing it in 1930. His aim in writing it had been to bring some realism into the schoolbook description of American society, and to a great extent he succeeded. In one volume, *An Introduction to Problems of American Culture*, he discussed unemployment, the problems faced by new immigrants, class structure, consumerism, and the speedup of life in an industrial society. These questions had never before been dealt with extensively in any school text, and the frankness of his approach remains startling even today. Rugg is probably still the only text writer who has advocated national economic planning and who has used the word "Socialist" on the first page of a book. His series does not, however, advocate Socialism. The books are full of pieties about the need for American children to become "tolerant, understanding and cooperating citizens." The series sold very well in the thirties. It was used in school systems containing nearly half of all American children, and for almost a decade there were no complaints about it. In 1939, a chorus of protests suddenly broke out. The first was from the Advertising Federation of America, which was offended by Rugg's disparaging remarks about advertising; then the National Association of Manufacturers, the American Legion, and a columnist for the Hearst press joined in, calling the series Socialist or Communist propaganda. The charges caught on and spread to community groups across the country. Dr. Rugg went on an extensive lecture tour to defend the series, during which he announced publicly that he was neither a Communist nor a Socialist. But in vain. A number of school boards banned the books, and others simply took them out of circulation. In 1938, the Rugg books sold 289,000 copies; in 1944, they sold only 21,000 copies; not long afterward, they disappeared from the market altogether.[17]

During the forties, business associations and right-wing citizens' groups attacked a number of other liberal textbooks and maintained a high level of pressure on the publishers. By 1950 or so, the merely conservative groups had been so successful that they had nothing more to complain about: the texts had become reflections of the National Association of Manufacturers viewpoint. This surrender by the publishers did not, however, end the war; it merely moved the battle lines farther to the right. In the mid-fifties, the anti-fluoridation lobby went on the offensive, followed a few years later by the John Birch Society, which — quite imaginatively — blamed the textbooks for the North Koreans' success in "brainwashing" a handful of American prisoners of war.[18] The textbook publishers took this seriously, for by that time they were so sensitive to right-wing pressure that they were checking their books before publication with a member of the Indiana State Textbook Commission named Ada White. Mrs. White believed, among other things, that Robin Hood was a Communist, and she urged that books that told the Robin Hood story be banned from Indiana schools. The publishers were no less mindful of the Texas State House of Representatives, which — in a state that already required a loyalty oath from all textbook writers — approved a resolution urging that "the American history courses in the public schools emphasize in the textbooks our glowing and throbbing history of hearts and souls inspired by wonderful American principles and traditions."[19]

The mid-sixties must have been a bewildering period for the textbook companies. In the space of a year or two, the political wind veered a hundred and eighty degrees. For the first time in publishing history, large-scale protests came from the left and from non-white people, and for the first time such protests were listened to. The turnaround began with a decision made by the Detroit Board of Education. In 1962, the local branch of the N.A.A.C.P. charged that one history text, published by Laidlaw Brothers, depicted slavery in a favorable light, and called on the Detroit board to withdraw it from the city school system. The N.A.A.C.P. and other civil-rights organizations had denounced racial prejudice in the textbooks a number of times in prior years with no real effect. This time, however, the Detroit board withdrew the text, and subsequently began to examine for racial bias all the history texts used in the school system. The Newark Textbook Council soon followed suit.[20] The movement then spread to other big-city school systems and was taken up by organizations representing other racial and ethnic minority groups — Mexican-Americans, Puerto Ricans, American Indians, Asian-Americans, Armenian-Americans, and so on — all of whom claimed, with justice, to have been ignored or abused by the textbooks. Within a few years, a dozen organizations, from the B'nai B'rith's Anti-Defamation League to a new Council on Interracial Books, were studying texts for racial, ethnic, and religious bias and making recommendations for a new generation of texts. What began as a series of discreet protests against individual books became a general proposition: all texts had treated the United States as a white, middle-class society when it was in fact multiracial and multicultural. And this proposition, never so much as suggested before 1962, had by the late sixties come to be a truism for the educational establishment.

The causes of this sudden upsurge of protest and the equally sudden change of perspective among educators are easy to understand in retrospect. As a result of the migrations from South to North during and after the Second World War, black Americans had become by the sixties a strong minority of the population in many Northern cities. In Detroit and Newark, they had become a majority. At the same time, the civil-rights movement had begun to focus national attention on the ugly facts of racial discrimination and prejudice in all areas of American life. A need for a change in the depiction of blacks and other minorities in textbooks, on television, and in advertising was merely one of the themes of the civil-rights movement, but it was the one that was the easiest to deal with. White Americans could resist racial integration in employment, in housing, and in the schools, but no one could deny the minorities at least a token place in the picture of American society. There was no principle to support a counter-argument, and, more important, no reason to make one. An alteration in the symbols could be made without any change in the reality.

The abrupt reversal of perspective in the schools created some panic in the textbook houses. Three or four years — the time it usually takes to produce a new basic text — seemed like an aeon relative to the change in consciousness. A single year was enough to outdate any given picture of America, and nobody could know what the next change would be. (On the evidence of one elementary-school social-studies text, the panic must have reached an all-time high at Noble & Noble. As late as 1964, *New York: Past and Present* made only fleeting reference to blacks. Two years later, another Noble & Noble book, *The New York Story*, included five chapters on blacks.)[21] No sooner had the editors begun to paste in pictures of Ralph Bunche and write reports on the civil-rights movement than along came the women's movement, sending them quite literally back to the drawing board — this time to change their representation of half the human species.

Only in the mid-seventies did the rate of change slow and the positions harden enough for the publishers to write guidelines for authors and editors on the treatment of racial and other minorities in the textbooks. These guidelines — which have since been published and thus set fast, at least for a while — give instructions on such things as the percentage of illustrations to be devoted to the various groups, and ways to avoid stereotyping in text or pictures.

The most interesting thing about them is the rather substantial modifications they make in the English language. The Holt, Rinehart & Winston guidelines on gender, for instance, include such strictures as "Avoid 'the founding fathers,' use 'the founders.' " (Holt also says, "Men are to be shown participating in a variety of domestic chores, such as cooking, sewing, housework, child-rearing, etc. Care should be taken to avoid implying that they are inept at these activities.")[22] Houghton Mifflin advises its editors to make sparing use of quoted material with male references, such as "These are the times that try men's souls"; it has discouraged the use of "the fatherland" and female pronouns referring to boats. To avoid ethnic stereotyping, its guidelines warn against the overuse of names like "Mary" and "John" and the use of only one ethnic name in lists of arbitrarily chosen names.[23] Macmillan, for its part, urges its editors not to transform ordinary words into negative concepts by adding "black" to them, as in "black market," and it gives "native Americans" as an alternative term for American Indians. There is, as the editors recognize, a certain arbitrariness about these decisions on usage.[24] Allyn & Bacon, for instance, subscribes to "native Americans" but not to "Hispanic-Americans." "We won't use the term Hispanic-Americans," one editor told me, "unless, of course, that becomes the way to go."

As the sixties ended, the publishers may have thought they had found some peace. But it was not to be. Just as soon as their guidelines were issued and pictures of female mechanics and native-American chairpersons began to appear in the books, the reaction set in. The demonstrations in Kanawha County were followed by a spate of smaller-scale protests in communities across the country. Then the John Birch Society emerged from a decade of near-silence to direct or help along (it was difficult to tell which) demonstrations in Washington against one of the new federally funded social-studies programs. Some of the protesters were merely registering conservative objections to what they saw as the excesses of the sixties; others went further, and attacked the whole drive for racial equality and women's rights.

More than automobile manufacturers or toothpaste executives, textbook publishers see themselves as beleaguered, even persecuted, people. And there is some justice in this view, for textbooks have become the lightning rods of American society. In the past, public protest over textbooks occurred only in times of rapid political or social change. Now a great number of organizations and informal groups take an interest in the content of texts. In addition to the racial and ethnic organizations, many of which disagree on what constitutes a "fair and accurate representation" of any given group, a multitude of educational and civil-rights groups have research departments devoted exclusively to the analysis of textbooks. Many of these departments — on the right and on the left — have with experience become sophisticated both in their analyses of text materials and in their methods of approaching publishers, school boards, and the federal bureaucracy. The public battle over texts is thus more intense and more complicated than it has ever been before. At the same time, the publishers have become much more sensitive to the market. Having availed themselves of many of the new market-research techniques, they can now register not just the great upheavals in society but also the slight tremors. They find this a mixed blessing. On the one hand, there are fewer surprises; on the other hand, they have had to become horrendously self-conscious. Does this math text have enough Polish-sounding people buying oranges? Does that third-grade reader show a woman fireperson? What will play in New York that will not offend the sensibilities of Peoria? As the publishers well know, it is impossible to satisfy everyone — or anyone for a long period.

There is perhaps only one group left in the country which does not bother the publishers — or anyway not very often — and that is the academic community. True, scholars do help "develop" textbooks, and occasionally they are permitted to have a significant role in determining their content. In the nineteen-sixties, the federal government was spending large sums for the development of new teaching materials, and groups of scholars selected by the learned societies developed a new generation of textbooks in the natural and social sciences. (The history texts, however, were not affected, for the American Historical Association did not take part.) But most scholars do not take secondary-school (or even college) textbooks seriously — not even when they have a hand in writing them. They do not make a practice of reading textbooks in their field, and no academic journal reviews textbooks on a regular basis. One consequence is that new scholarship trickles down extremely slowly into the school texts; as it proceeds, usually by way of the college texts, the elapsed time between the moment an idea or an approach gains currency in the academic community and the moment it reaches the school texts may be fifteen years or more. Another consequence is that there is no real check on the intellectual quality — or even the factual accuracy — of school textbooks. The result is that on the scale of publishing priorities the pursuit of truth appears somewhere near the bottom.

In a perfectly democratic, or custom-designed, world,

every teacher would be allowed to choose his or her own history textbook—which is to say that the publishing houses would publish books in a variety large enough to suit all tastes. But this has somehow never happened, in spite of all the structural changes the textbook business has undergone in the United States over the past hundred years. The late nineteenth century ought to have been the period for a great diversity of books, because scores of publishers were competing then in a burgeoning school market. At the time, however, the content of texts was the least of a publisher's worries, for—particularly in the West, where the competition was the most intense—the sale of books depended largely on which company could most successfully bribe or otherwise corrupt the whiskey dealers, preachers, and political-party hacks who sat on the school boards. This degree of free enterprise proved uneconomical in the long run. In the eighteen-nineties, three of the major companies banded together to form the American Book Company, which acquired a seventy-five- to eighty-per-cent monopoly of the textbook market. Yet this streamlining of the industry did not make for a wider selection of books. Indeed, when the American Book Company acquired a total monopoly in geography publishing, it produced no new books in that field for many years.[25] Competition was eventually reëstablished, and there was some greater variety in the texts until the ideological freeze of the Cold War. In recent years, the industry has been a model of American free enterprise: four hundred companies (forty of them major ones) have competed fiercely, but with a fairly high degree of probity, to sell more or less the same product to the same people.

In the mid-sixties, there were high hopes in the publishing industry that this situation would change. Sitting at the feet of Marshall McLuhan, the publishers decided that the era of mass production was over — along with the era of literacy and linear reasoning — and that they should at once prepare to deliver instant all-around audiovisual programming with individualized feedback for every child. The era of software had come — the era of total communication and perfect customization. Not only — or even principally — the textbook publishers but a lot of high-rolling communications-industry executives dreamed of equipping every classroom in America with television sets, video cameras, holography sets, and computer terminals. As a first step toward this post-industrial future, the executives built conglomerates designed to put all kinds of software components and communications capability under one roof. Xerox acquired Ginn & Company; RCA bought Random House; C.B.S. acquired Holt, Rinehart & Winston; Raytheon bought D. C. Heath; and Time Inc. acquired Little, Brown and Company and Silver Burdett and, with General Electric, formed the General Learning Corporation.

The problem was that all the new theories about education, information, and business in the future rested on the availability of large-scale government funding, a growing student population, and a ballooning economy. And none of these conditions held for very long. As soon as the costs of the Vietnam War came home, the schools drastically curtailed their multimedia programs, the government cut back funding of research projects to develop new teaching methods and materials, and the conglomerates began to look like no more than the sum of their parts. And then, with great speed, fashions changed, and educational theory turned conservative. Parents and school boards complained that children couldn't read or write anymore

— that what they needed was textbook drill. Publishers, up to their ears in machinery, began to look on textbooks as the basic winter coat. While they continued to produce some of the cheapest of the new materials — such things as magazines and filmstrips — they put their money back into books: both the hardbacks and a new generation of paperbacks, which allowed teachers a choice of supplementary material. "It began to dawn on them," one trade-book editor says, "that the book is finally the most efficient retrieval system we possess."

The big basic history textbook thus seems here to stay, at least for a bit, and to stay just about what it has always been in this century — a kind of lowest common denominator of American tastes. The books of the seventies are somewhat more diverse than those of the fifties, but still they differ from one another not much more than one year's crop of Detroit sedans. This is hardly surprising, since, like cars, textbooks are expensive to design and relatively cheap to duplicate. The development of a new eleventh-grade history text can cost five hundred thousand dollars (more this year, perhaps), with an additional hundred thousand in marketing costs. Since the public schools across the country now spend less than one per cent of their budgets on buying books (textbook publishing is only a seven-hundred-million-dollar-a-year business),[26] publishers cannot afford to have more than one or two basic histories on the market at the same time. Consequently, all of them try to compete for the center of the market, designing their books not to please anyone in particular but to be acceptable to as many people as possible. The word "controversial" is as deeply feared by textbook publishers as it is coveted by trade-book publishers. What a textbook reflects is thus a compromise, an America sculpted and sanded down by the pressures of diverse constituents and interest groups.

History textbooks for elementary and secondary schools are not like other kinds of histories. They serve a different function, and they have their own traditions, which continue independent of academic history writing. In the first place, they are essentially nationalistic histories. The first American-history text was written after the American Revolution, and because of it; and most texts are still accounts of the nation-state. In the second place, they are written not to explore but to instruct — to tell children what their elders want them to know about their country. This information is not necessarily what anyone considers the truth of things. Like time capsules, the texts contain the truths selected for posterity.

The surprise is how quickly and how thoroughly these truths for posterity have changed. And the changes have occurred not only in the past two or three decades. To read the texts published over the two hundred years of United States history is to see several complete revisions in the picture they present of the country and its place in the world. These apparently solid, authoritative tomes are in fact the most nervous of objects, constantly changing in style as well as in political content. In the nineteenth century, when the texts usually had identifiable authors, the changes could be measured in generations; in the early twentieth century, they occurred in every decade. Since the nineteen-forties, however, the practice of rewriting texts every few years has meant that children who belong to the same generation often get very different impressions of the national identity.

American-history texts gained general currency in the

schools only in the eighteen-nineties. Before then, American history was not very widely taught. The public grade schools had very little history of any kind in their curricula, and the private academies that prepared students for colleges and universities concentrated on classical studies and European history. The place that American-history texts now hold as the common element in children's schooling belonged in the nineteenth century to Noah Webster's spellers and rhetoric books, and then to the McGuffey readers. The Webster and McGuffey books had snatches of American history between their catechisms and their stories, but their bent was literary, and, apart from teaching children how to read, they taught mostly manners and morals. That fact suggests that until the eighteen-nineties Americans thought of themselves as belonging to a particular culture and holding certain values; they defined themselves by that culture much more than by the fact of the nation-state. The early-nineteenth-century history texts seem to bear this proposition out, since none of them offered much information on government, on politics, or even on the shape of the country. Samuel Goodrich, who, under the name of Peter Parley, published some of the most popular of all the pre–Civil War school histories, added large quantities of pure fiction to what was an otherwise unrelieved account of earthquakes and other natural disasters. His tales about the heroism of little boys in Indian raids were there not just to make good reading but to provide moral instruction for the student.

The first school historians of the United States did not lack patriotic ardor, but they seemed to lack a means of expressing it. New England clergymen for the most part, they suffered from the circumstances that before the Revolution American history was not a proper subject for study and therefore they had little education in it. But instead of trying to compensate for this deficiency they tended to make things up. The Reverend Jedidiah Morse, a friend of Noah Webster's and the first American school geographer, wrote, for instance, "North America has no remarkably high mountains. The most considerable are . . . the Allegheny Mountains."[27] Then, the American history they eventually wrote seemed to have very little to do with the morality they professed for it. Goodrich's more factual-minded successors concerned themselves almost entirely with violence and with events of the nature of man-bites-dog. Emma Willard, a pioneer in the education of women in the United States, wrote in the foreword to one of her histories (published in 1847) that students should study history in order to increase their virtue, and that American history was particularly appropriate in this regard, because "in comparison with these old and wily nations, the character of America is that of youthful simplicity, of maiden purity."[28] Her text, however, describes an almost uninterrupted sequence of massacres, rebellions, Indian attacks, border skirmishes, and major wars (the wars drawn out for pages, battle by battle). In these sanguinary conflicts, the only real virtue that Americans seem to have is the negative one of not behaving quite as despicably as everyone else.

Many of the nineteenth-century text writers had decided opinions on things. For example, they did not like foreigners at all, and they had a particularly keen dislike for the Spanish. The Reverend Mr. Morse wrote of the Spanish, "Naturally weak and effeminate, they dedicate the greatest part of their lives to loitering and inactive pleasures. Luxurious without variety or elegance, and expensive with great parade and little convenience, their character is nothing more than a grave and specious insignificance."[29] The prose style of these writers is unparalleled in the twentieth century, and, indeed, in many respects it is all downhill rhetorically from the heights of the Reverend Mr. Morse. Unfortunately, their sense of structure — their feeling for the flow of history — did not measure up to their style. They relied desperately on chronology, and some of them placed their evaluation of each President at a point in the text that corresponded to the date of the President's death, no matter how long the man had been out of office by then or what was currently going on. They told a lot of anecdotes, but these did not always advance the narrative line. One writer, for instance, reported that George Washington had introduced Lafayette to his mother at a ball after a certain battle, and that Lafayette had found the lady impressive. The story ends there. On the whole, their characterizations of historical figures, like their political analyses, tended to be thin.

The history texts of the eighteen-nineties appear at first glance to have originated in a different civilization from the one that produced the earlier texts. And that is more or less the case. The decade before the turn of the century brought, among other things, a transformation of the educational system. Since the Civil War, the number of public high schools had grown rapidly — to the point where the high schools now had more students than the private academies. While the state legislatures concerned themselves with the politics of this development (many of them started requiring courses in American history), the teachers and college professors organized national associations to set standards for the teaching profession and to bring some order to the secondary-school curriculum. This work of organization and standardization — such as was then taking place in all the professions — was accompanied by a certain change in philosophy about the nature of the scholarly enterprise. In the field of history, university professors under the influence of the German school began to explore problems of methodology and to conclude that if history was not a science (which many, such as Henry Adams, hoped it might turn out to be), then at least it was a discipline, and not just a craft practiced by men of leisure. This notion moved gradually into the schools and schoolbooks in the form of a general recognition that facts were important and certain facts more important than others.

The texts of the eighteen-nineties thus constitute a departure. In the first place, they are written in terse, declarative sentences — the so-called telegraphic style. In the second place, they are orderly to the point of compulsion. Gone are the old eccentricities of style and the old piling up of events on dates; their material is organized into themes, such as "The English Colonies" or "The Rise of Parties," the significance of each theme being stated as bluntly as possible in the chapter heading. The books give much less space to battles and much more to politics, economics, and governmental undertakings of all sorts. Institutions appear amid the welter of events — the formation of the Republic now has a significance equal to that of the Revolutionary War — and personalities are fleshed out slightly with description and pertinent anecdote. Finally, the books sound a new note of restraint. The authors clearly have their opinions, but they do not force them adjectivally upon their readers. The books have a tone of objectivity and authoritativeness. That tone is, of course, spurious — a pure formality. But seen in retrospect the assumption of this impersonal voice was as important an innovation in the history of textbooks as the discovery of perspective was in the history of painting. From the eighteen-nineties on, what the texts said about American history would appear to children to be the truth.

If the eighteen-nineties could be viewed as the Quattrocento of American-history text writing, then the period between 1910 and 1930 was surely the Renaissance of that particular form. In 1911, there appeared the first edition of David Saville Muzzey's *American History*; in 1913, the first work by the Progressive historian Willis Mason West. Subsequently, there were books by Charles and Mary Beard, by the Harvard historian Albert Bushnell Hart, and by a number of other first-rank historians, including Andrew C. McLaughlin and Wilbur Fisk Gordy. At the very end of the period, Harold Rugg began publishing his series. The new textbook authors were not simply writers for children, as the nineteenth-century authors usually were, but professors chosen for their academic distinction and for their ability to synthesize large issues for children. Some of them were considerable prose stylists, and though their texts do not have the same flair — or sometimes even the same point of view — as their less synthetic works, the new textbook convention of deadpan writing does not entirely filter out the sound of their individual voices.

Ideologically speaking, the books produced in this period were a good deal more diverse than those published in the eighteen-nineties — or, indeed, in any subsequent period until the late nineteen-sixties. Not only the authors of the books but, by and large, the new audience of secondary-school teachers belonged to the Progressive political movement, and believed in political and pedagogical reform. On the right end of the spectrum were Muzzey (of whom more later) and Hart, with their aristocratic New

England brand of Progressive politics. These gentlemen looked upon the Age of Enlightenment as the source of the best in the American tradition. They revered the Founding Fathers and, on their behalf, carried on the only serious attempt at ancestor worship in American textbook history. Hart argued, typically, "One evidence that the Revolution was justified is the fact that the best and ablest men in the colonies believed that their liberty was in danger. When Benjamin Franklin heartily joined in the war, there must have been reason for it."[30] For Hart and Muzzey, character was all-important, and the quality of individual leaders was the central issue in politics and in history. Hart, who disapproved of Western expansionist adventures in general, wrote, "The defect of Polk's character was his lack of moral principle as to the property of our neighbor, Mexico."[31]

On the left end of the spectrum between 1910 and 1920 was Willis Mason West. For West, the significant actors in history were not individuals but economic forces, social groups, and political institutions. West specifically disapproved of the New England view of the Enlightenment. The first of his books begins, "I have tried to correct the common delusion which looks back to Jefferson or John Winthrop for a golden age, and to show instead that democracy has as yet been tried only imperfectly among us." True to this purpose, West reports in the body of his text that the delegates to the Constitutional Convention did not believe in government by the people, that they belonged to the eighteenth century rather than to the twentieth, and that "they represented the crest of a reactionary movement of their own day."[32] West thought that the main value of the American Revolution lay in the fact that it opened up new opportunities to a great number of people and called forth new social energies. In writing about the late nineteenth century, West — almost alone among text writers — discussed class conflict and the "warlike" relationship between labor and capital. He was nonetheless something of a moralist, and he was a true Progressive in that he believed in salvation by the elevation of consciousness. In the conclusion of his 1913 text, he wrote of the Progressive period, "The Nation awoke shamed . . . enmeshed in a net of intangible chains. . . . Now at the end of another twenty years, a new dawn is breaking. The moral sense of the people has grown steadily more and more alert [We have] a gallant group of leaders . . . with weapons for the strife."[33]

These Progressive texts continued to appear throughout the twenties (textbooks being always somewhat behind the times), along with a number of conservative histories. None of the former were as politically explicit as the West book, but all carried at least some slight strain of dissent from prevailing institutions. Some of the thirties texts maintained this distance, even while introducing a very different style of political thinking. The more leftist among them reflected a hazy kind of Socialism — the ideology of the progressive-education movement, as opposed to that of the now-defunct Progressive Party. Perhaps in obedience to John Dewey's dictum that economic history is more democratic than political history, Charles Garrett Vannest and Henry Lester Smith collaborated on a text that is short on political history. Like Harold Rugg's civilization series, their *Socialized History of the United States* reports on the development of American society and tends to slight Presidents or other leaders. The approach did not result in any great narrative fluency. Of the Pilgrims, the book reports, "After a stormy voyage of over two months, they landed at Plymouth, where for the first few years they had a hard time."[34] But books such as this were clearly not meant for the entertainment of children. They were designed to promote social reform by indoctrinating children with tolerance, coöperation, and other social-democratic virtues.

What carried over from the thirties into the forties was this tone of high moral seriousness — little more. For the period of ideological diversity — the Hundred Flowers of textbook writing — ended abruptly with the beginning of the Second World War. The warning signal was the N.A.M.-sponsored attack on the Rugg series; even before that controversy ended, the publishers were dropping or revising all history texts of a similar nature and hiring new authors. Within a few years, there were no more dissenting books on the market. The political spectrum of the texts narrowed to a point somewhere in the neighborhood of Dwight D. Eisenhower and remained there for the next twenty-five years.

As might be expected, the texts of the forties give emphasis to political history, or, rather — since in many ways these texts deny the very existence of politics — to the history of government actions. The word "democracy" is not, as it was in the thirties books, a call to social action but simply the name of the American system, and the opposite of Fascism and Communism — which are not themselves very well defined. The curious thing about these books is that all of them insist upon the right to vote as the foundation stone of democracy. They do that in spite of the fact that this right exists in the Soviet Union and provides no real impediment to the rule of the Communist Party bureaucrats.

Unsurprisingly, the forties texts show a new interest in

foreign affairs. In addition to a rather belated concern for Europe, they manifest a sudden rush of enthusiasm for Latin America. This enthusiasm lasts exactly as long as President Franklin D. Roosevelt's Good Neighbor Policy, leaving only one sign of its passage: the word "imperialism," which was once freely used to describe United States adventures in Asia and the Caribbean at the end of the nineteenth century, no longer applies to the United States. According to these books, imperialism is a European affair: "we" have a Monroe Doctrine and a Good Neighbor Policy. The words "we" and "our" crop up frequently in the forties texts — most prominently in the titles. Whereas the twenties books are usually called something like *An American History* or *The History of the United States* (the naming of texts never having been an occasion for much originality), those of the forties have such titles as *The Story of America* and *The Story of Our Republic*, the implication of which is that the student must identify with everything that has ever happened in American history.

In the fifties, these concerns do not so much change as intensify. The morbid fear of Communism becomes an overriding passion — to the point where in some books the whole of American history appears a mere prologue to the struggle with the "Reds." Most books devote more than half of their twentieth-century history to foreign affairs and focus their attention on the question of "how the United States became a world power." American power and strength are the leitmotivs of these books. Even the War of 1812, which ended — to put the matter in its best light — in a military standoff, appears as yet another victory in the triumphal march of America. After 1914, "we" are, according to the texts, "taking up our responsibilities" for the rest of the world. There is a fascination with patriotic symbols — the flag, Independence Hall, the Statue of Liberty. And the static, legalistic quality of the political analysis in the forties books has now hardened into a neo-Confucian mold, wherein the American political system appears eternal and unchanging. One of the major texts of the period, Henry W. Bragdon and Samuel P. McCutchen's *History of a Free People*, concludes with an essay extolling the virtues of freedom not for its own sake but merely as the greatest asset in the world struggle.

For all their insistence on the wealth, strength, and virtue of the United States, the fifties texts do not have a very sunny view of the future. In the concluding sections, there are a good many grim warnings that citizens must do jury duty, pay taxes, and learn to recognize hostile propaganda. Children are also repeatedly informed that their liberties will disappear if they do not defend them properly. This, the books invariably conclude, is the most difficult and challenging period in American history. Even the sections on the wonders of science are not particularly reassuring, for where the thirties books looked forward to improvements in society and human nature, these look forward to progress only in an inhuman sphere beyond most people's control.

The texts of the fifties are notable for laying equal stress on political, social, and economic history. They give the development of American industry — a subject that was sorely neglected by their predecessors — an important place in nineteenth-century history. And while they tend to side with the Pinkertons against the labor radicals, they give nineteenth-century labor-union history as much space as they give the captains of industry. What is missing from their economic history is, first, a description of the structural changes in the American economy since the eighteen-thirties and, second, an account of how these structural changes affected American politics. But the same might be said of their political and social history: the books do not describe change or show the relationship between one kind of event and another. The nineteen-fifties texts are encyclopedias rather than history books. Their vast indexes contain references to everything under the sun, but there is no connection between one thing and another. Events stand isolated below headings of black type, like islands in some archipelago where no one has yet invented the canoe.

The texts of the sixties contain the most dramatic rewriting of history ever to take place in American schoolbooks. The political alteration began in 1965, when texts first reported the assassination of President Kennedy. From then on, problems of a new sort begin to crop up. At first, these problems are confined to the concluding sections; they come apparently from nowhere, since if one believes the rest of the books the United States, threatened though it may be from the outside, has a just and pacific society and a firm but peaceable foreign policy. Later, these problems multiply, and they spread like measles through the texts. The late-sixties editions show that foreign policy has been a problem for years, what with Suez and the Cuban missile crisis and other such challenges. Urban blight, too, has long been a problem, and black Americans have historically been discriminated against. By the early seventies, these problems are running rampant through American history; indeed, according to one book, American history is "a gnarled experience involving problems, turmoil, and conflict." Then, even while the problems are still breaking out, there is a distinct shift of emphasis from foreign policy to domestic social history. Blacks and other minority groups enter the books slowly, their way prepared by George Washington Carver. At the same time, the static, neo-Confucian style gives way to a somewhat more dynamic — or simply historical — mode of political analysis. These changes in interpretation bring with them new sets of facts or, as in the case of Reconstruction, the old set of facts used backward. To read all the editions of the sixties texts is thus a bewildering experience. What changes is nothing less than the character of the United States.

A survey of the books published in the successive decades of the twentieth century might seem to show that the students of each decade have grown up with a completely different version of American history. But this is not entirely true. For nearly half the century, a high percentage — perhaps even a majority — of American schoolchildren learned American history from a single book: David Saville Muzzey's *American History*. In one of the most competitive of markets, Muzzey's *American History* survived for sixty-five years, selling more copies for much of that time than any of its competitors — and in certain periods more than all of them combined — and proving almost as popular in the days of the jet aircraft as in those of the horse-drawn carriage. First published in 1911, it became an immediate best-seller. It continued to top the lists in the nineteen-thirties. And it went on selling strongly through the forties and fifties, its popularity waning only in the early sixties. In the mid-seventies, it was still in print and still serving as the history text for thousands of students. For staying power, the book is matched only by *Magruder's American Government*, which, now in its sixty-second year, covers more than fifty per cent of the market for government texts. But whereas "Magruder" is more or less a reference book — an encyclopedia of American-government institutions, revised and updated every year — Muzzey is a narrative history that was written by one man and changed remarkably little from the time of its first publication until its author's death, in the nineteen-sixties.

Ask the editors at Ginn & Company to explain the phenomenal success of the book and they will say, "Muzzey wrote well for children," and then shrug. They are right to be diffident, for the book has no single quality that sets it off from all other texts — except, perhaps, its style. It is not a formula book; on the contrary, even after half a century of editorial sandpapering it remains personal, even slightly eccentric. The views it expresses do not derive from any single, orthodox system; rather, they reflect a whole person with a unique sensibility and a not altogether tidy outlook on the world. What made this personality so attractive to several generations of Americans? It is better to turn the question around, since there is clearly a mystery in it. To examine the book closely is to learn something new about those generations of Americans.

The Ginn editors are right: Muzzey is well written. In comparison with other history texts, it is wonderfully lively and colorful. The vocabulary is large, and the images are unconventional. Verbs always carry the sentences, and the sentences are varied enough to create nice changes of rhythm. Not only the prose is lively — so is the world that Muzzey creates for children. His history is full of characters — people with beliefs, emotions, and voices of their own. There is a good deal of scenery, very few abstractions, and many wonderful stories. Describing the assassination of Lincoln, Muzzey reports that "as Booth leaped down onto the stage after firing his fatal shot, his spur caught in the folds of the American flag which decorated the Presidential box, and he fell, breaking his leg. He made his escape from the theatre on a horse that was waiting at the stage door, but was soon afterward trapped in a barn in Virginia and shot." Clearly, Muzzey did not see history as something that was dead or that was useless except insofar as it explained "present conditions." Indeed, from the theatrical images he uses in his first editions ("stages" are constantly "being set," and "curtains" are "rising" or "falling"), it is clear that he saw history as a series of terrific dramas. He had heroes ("the great commander, Washington") and villains ("the unspeakable demagogue" Benjamin F. Butler), each of whom had his own intrinsic interest as a person.

Probably almost none of the teachers or students who used Muzzey's text knew anything about the man (few dictionaries of national biography so much as mention him), but they might have guessed something of his background from the text itself. David Saville Muzzey came, as it happened, from Massachusetts — from the state with the strongest tradition of public education. His family was of pre-Revolutionary vintage, and among his forebears, one of whom had owned Lexington Green, were members of the old intellectual élite of teachers and preachers. Born in 1870, Muzzey as a young man had studied at Union Theological Seminary before deciding on the other course of becoming a historian. He then went to the Sorbonne and the University of Berlin; back in the United States, he studied with James Harvey Robinson, one of the distinguished historians who at the turn of the century helped to bring the more exacting standards of European scholarship to the United States. He became a professor at Columbia University and for many years taught an American-history class at the Ethical Culture Schools.

In the preface to the 1936 edition of his text, Muzzey wrote:

> Each of you should think of himself or herself as a person who has inherited a beautiful country estate, and should be proud to keep up that estate and to make such "modern improvements" as will increase its beauty and comforts. You would be ungrateful heirs indeed if you did not care to know who had bequeathed the estate to you, who had planned and built the house [and defended] it from marauders and burglars.

Muzzey was speaking metaphorically, but he clearly had a certain kind of reader in mind. He was also, as it happened, describing himself and some of the most profound attitudes and assumptions in his book. As the text alone makes quite clear, he not only believed in the value of history but — unlike many Americans — felt himself to be a legitimate heir to it. "We," he wrote in the 1911 edition, identifying himself with the United States government. His book is filled with confident judgments not only on matters of fact but on the wisdom and morality of national enterprises. For instance, he judged the 1848 war with Mexico to have been wrong, because it intensified the debate over slavery and so proved to be another source of North-South strife. "The fruits of the Mexican war," he wrote, in one of his more highly colored passages, "like the apples of Sodom, turned to ashes in our mouth."[35]

As the 1936 preface also implies, Muzzey had very definite class attitudes. In the 1911 edition, for instance, he described Shays' Rebellion from the point of view of the

Massachusetts merchants and manufacturers who "had to subdue an armed mob of 1500 rebels of the debtor class."[36] A Progressive on contemporary social issues, he felt it "inconceivable that the great body of American citizens . . . will long allow one tenth of their number to stagnate in abject poverty."[37] That he despised poverty did not, however, mean that he identified with the poor. The mass of poor immigrants who had arrived around the end of the century were "they" to him — aliens whom "we" had to "assimilate and mold into citizenship," lest they become "an undigested and indigestible element in our body politic, and a constant menace to our free institutions."[38] For him, "Americans" — real Americans — were not a mass but individuals; they were people like himself, of English descent, with traditions of independent landed wealth and a genteel culture.

From Muzzey's identification with England many things followed. In the first place, he anchored American history firmly in Europe, and American politics in the British political tradition. This acknowledgment of parentage was not conventional wisdom; many of the nineteenth-century texts credited the United States with what amounted to a virgin birth. He viewed the Revolution as a separation from, rather than a rejection of, Europe, and saw the War of 1812 as unnecessary and unfortunate, in part because it benefitted Napoleon. So strong was his European orientation that he knew and cared very little about the American West. He had no sympathy with the war hawks or the proponents of Manifest Destiny. California was a blank on his map; indeed, apart from the frontiersmen and covered-wagon settlers the whole country west of Chicago did not really exist for him. In all editions of the book, he was lukewarm about American imperial adventures in the Caribbean and in Asia. On the other hand, he was an internationalist with regard to Europe, favoring American intervention in the two world wars and participation in the League of Nations and the United Nations. Interestingly, the 1955 edition is not half so stridently anti-Communist as the other texts of that period. It is anti-Soviet, but that is all. China does not get "lost" until the 1963 edition — a version that was revised by another historian.

With regard to the Civil War, Muzzey declared himself firmly for the Union side and the policies of Lincoln. He thought slavery an evil, but, like some of his colleagues at Columbia University, he looked upon Reconstruction from the perspective of the white Southern gentry. President Andrew Johnson was "coarse, violent, egotistical, obstinate, and vindictive," but the Radical Republicans (including "the unspeakable demagogue" Butler) were a good deal worse. Indeed, there was nothing good about Reconstruction — not even the Fourteenth and Fifteenth Amendments, since the enfranchisement of the freedmen "set the ignorant, superstitious, gullible slave in power over his former master." Muzzey moderated his language a bit in later editions, but he continued to insist that the situation in the South improved only in 1877, when "the Southern people were given charge of their own government."[39] Not until the 1961 edition did the book suggest that blacks might be numbered among the "Southern people," and then only by virtue of some rather condescending words about Tuskegee and Booker T. Washington.

On the subject of race, Muzzey held the view, conventional in the early part of the century, that each race had its own innate moral character, and that some races were simply inferior to others. The Aztecs, for instance, were sunk in "moral degradation"; the North American Indians "had some noble qualities . . . but at bottom they were a treacherous, cruel people."[40] The Negro was lazy and had to be protected by the white man. In the earlier editions, there is some confusion between race and nationality, as in "the English race"; this disappears later on, but what remains is the definition of race as culture and as moral personality. This view, which was common in the Progressive era, derived from nineteenth-century science, with its presumption of innate "character," and it was this nineteenth-century racism that Muzzey's book taught generations of twentieth-century children.

Muzzey's conception of democracy and his philosophy of history seemed to come from an even earlier time. The liveliness of his writing resulted in no small part from the fact that he portrayed individual leaders — George Washington and George III — as free agents, whose vices and virtues determined the course of history. History was for him a personal matter. He wrote of sectional-interest and economic-interest groups, but with disapproval. His ideal of government was a debate between such figures as Clay and Calhoun. It is for this reason that, among Presidents, he adored Washington and Jefferson, respected John Quincy Adams, and disliked Andrew Jackson, whom he thought arrogant and uncouth. (Jackson became a hero of frontier democracy only in the 1961 edition.) Also for this reason, he despised or ignored all the Presidents — except Hayes and Cleveland — who held office between the Civil War and the end of the century. His twentieth-century hero was Theodore Roosevelt.

As might be imagined, Muzzey's weak point as a historian — his blind spot, in fact — was economic and social history. He simply could not see the drama of the American Industrial Revolution; he could not describe the violent change in the culture which accompanied it. In the first edition, he went so far as to apologize to his readers for "the lack of romantic elements in an economic age" and to complain of the "lack of moral fervour" in the period between 1865 and 1900.[41] He hated the anarchic capitalism of the period — the major problem of his own time, he felt, was "the corruption of the government by the money power" — but he was hardly able to write about Rockefeller or Carnegie at all. In the 1955 edition, Muzzey or his surrogates the Ginn editors actually project upon the "captains of industry" a desire to develop natural resources (as opposed to the simple desire to make money) — a motive that Muzzey himself would have considered proper. The blank he draws on the labor movement is even more nearly complete. In the 1911 edition, he makes one mention of what he calls "the laboring class"; in subsequent editions, he gives the obligatory page or two to the development of the unions. But his interest in the unions never went much beyond his fear of social disruption. To him, all organizations to the left of the American Federation of Labor were hotbeds of foreign agitators preaching anarchism or Bolshevism. As time went on, therefore, events became more and more difficult for Muzzey to describe or explain. He hated the twenties and thirties, for their combination of isolationism in foreign policy and "industrial chaos, social ferment, class struggle, bitter propaganda, commercial profiteering, and reckless business plunging" at home. He could not explain the Depression or the New Deal, and only the Second World War seemed to make him feel that the country was once again engaged in a noble cause.

From the perspective of the nineteen-seventies, Muzzey seems in many ways a contradictory figure. On the one hand, he had the instincts of a reformer. The concluding sections of his texts are lists of "problems" facing the United States. These problems include the domination of the government by the great trusts, the waste of natural resources, commercialism, the poverty of one-tenth of the population, and — in the nineteen-thirties — bad race relations. On the other hand, he was a reactionary when it came to organized-labor politics. The solutions he proposed to these problems never involved institutional change but only an amorphous moral regeneration. "The manhood of the nation must rise in its moral strength to restore our democratic institutions" — that sort of thing.

A possible explanation of Muzzey's politics is to be found in Richard Hofstadter's *The Age of Reform*. In his book on the Progressive period, Hofstadter identified a group of Mugwump leaders who later became an important element in the Progressive Party:

> Protestant and Anglo-Saxon for the most part, they were very frequently of New England ancestry; and even when they were not, they tended to look to New England's history for literary, cultural and political models and for examples of moral idealism. . . . Their ideal leader was a well-to-do, well-educated, high-minded citizen, rich enough to be free from motives of what they often called "crass materialism."[42]

Hofstadter quotes Alfred D. Chandler, Jr., as saying that these men were "individualists, unacquainted with institutional discipline [who] represented, in spite of their thoroughly urban backgrounds, the ideas of the older, more rural America." These men, Hofstadter explains, saw themselves as Enlightenment figures. Like Henry Adams, they believed in the powers of altruism and the rule of law.

And they looked upon government as an ally against the corruption and social chaos that attended the rapid industrialization of the country. As they saw it, the Progressive reform movement promised a restoration of Jeffersonian democracy and of the power of the individual over the interests, capital and labor included. That this ideal individual bore a close resemblance to a middle-class professional of their own sort was, Hofstadter submits, no coincidence, since their main social grievance was the sudden decline of their own status relative to that of the new industrial plutocracy. They legislated reforms, but they could never make common cause with the immigrants, because they looked a century back, to the society in which they had dominant wealth and influence. In a sense, they were not progressives at all but thoroughgoing reactionaries.

Just why Muzzey's textbook — and this very particular world view of a New England gentleman — should have been so attractive to Americans for fifty years is an interesting question to speculate upon. The book was, after all, read by people of all ethnic backgrounds, and its popularity endured through three major ideological shifts in the country. A part of the attraction may have been Muzzey's tone of self-assurance, his assumption of his own legitimacy in the American tradition. For Westerners and people of less ancient American ancestry than he, Muzzey may have seemed to be the voice of the real America — the America they wanted to, or felt they should, belong to. Another possible explanation — and the two are not mutually exclusive — is that the Mugwumps expressed one of the most deep-seated of American political instincts: if not a majority of Americans, then a controlling proportion believes optimistically that the country can right its own wrongs without a change in the institutional structure. Americans believe in the politics of good will.

A third possibility — and, again, a complementary one — is that it is far easier to teach children élite politics than politics of any other kind. Children, after all, cannot learn politics the way they learn mathematics or French; they must have some experience of life to understand how societies work, and the workings of democracies are far more difficult to grasp than those of monarchies or dictatorships. The difficulty is not just intellectual but aesthetic as well. Histories in which the main actors are institutions or social forces tend to lack surface attraction — an immediate appeal to the emotions. There is far more natural drama in the biographical mode — and Muzzey exploited it to the full. What this suggests is that Dewey and his many successors, who advocated teaching a truly democratic history, may have been fighting an uphill battle for the minds of young people.

The Muzzey phenomenon is unique. Even now, nearly twenty years after his *American History* lost its hold on the market, no American-history text has come anywhere near its popularity or anywhere near its sales relative to other textbooks. While there may be a number of reasons for this, one important one is the change in textbook-publishing procedures. The textbook companies and beyond them the school boards simply do not permit authors the freedom to write their own books in their own way. Today, texts are written backward or inside out, as it were, beginning with public demand and ending with the historian. This system gives the publishers a certain security, since their books cannot be too far out of the mainstream. But, having minimized one kind of risk, they have created another, of a different order. By casting away scholarly claims to authority, they have set themselves adrift on the uncertain seas of public opinion. The voyage can be uncomfortable at times. It is difficult when opinions are divided or are changing rapidly, and it is just as difficult when, as happens quite frequently, people do not really know what they want to hear. For the past ten years, the publishers have suffered from both of these conditions.

✦

Continuity and Change

Also Breakdowns, Hairpin Turns, and Roads Not Taken

✦

WHAT is remarkable about the American-history texts of the late sixties and early seventies compared with those of the past is the sense of uncertainty they show. The central questions of American history — Is there such a thing as an American identity? What kind of society does the United States have? What are American values? What position does the United States occupy in the world? — are disputed territory for them, as they were not for their predecessors. Of course, the question of national identity is not the easiest of subjects to deal with, but, since the American Revolution, text writers, unlike most historians and novelists, have always succeeded in painting a fairly simple picture of America. Even while the country was changing radically in shape, in population, and even in looks, they had definite answers to the questions about who and what we were. These answers changed over time, but at any given moment they were remarkably uniform and remarkably simple. The shattering of this single image in current texts thus constitutes an important break with tradition. But the break is not yet complete, and it is that which makes them so confusing. Modern text writers, after all, have to deal not only with current realities but with the very powerful images of America that their predecessors taught generations of Americans.

Until the twentieth century, few American educators believed that textbooks — or schooling in general — could or should be an instrument for changing the culture. Those textbook writers who saw their books as something more than a representation of the world believed that they should be a force for conservation. The one powerful exception was Noah Webster. In the wake of the Revolution, Webster took up the enterprise of writing a new dictionary and new spellers and readers for the express purpose of changing the country. His ambition in making replacements for the British texts was to do for American culture what the Revolution had done for American politics. A true radical, he believed that this meant not just separation but liberation. Through his books, he aimed at cutting the American language loose from its moorings in English speech and setting it free to pursue its own development, in the course of which it would eventually grow as different from English as Dutch is from German. But there was a contradictory quality to his whole enterprise. His hopes for the language were never realized, and this was at least in part because of his own success in standardizing it at a point where it was not really very different from English. His ambition conflicted in the sphere of values as well, for while Webster was a nationalist, he was also intensely, and increasingly, conservative. Like Jefferson, Franklin, and others of the Revolutionary generation, he defined America and Americans by contrasting them with the nations of Europe. Europe was the Old World; America was the New. Europeans were luxury-loving, deceitful, and corrupt, their societies divided by extremes of wealth and poverty; Americans were all honest yeomen farmers dressed in homespun — sober, industrious, and practical. Thus, Americans were anything but experimental or iconoclastic. And it was Webster's conservatism, not his radicalism, that became the dominant force in American education for most of the nineteenth century.

The conservative instincts of American educators — so strange in a new country — resulted in large part from the fact that at the time of the Revolution education remained within the purview of religious schools. Webster's image of Americans was in fact the traditional, Puritan one, and it survived mainly because for the first half of the nineteenth century there was little change in the school system. Most of the early writers of American-history textbooks were preachers or teachers in church schools, and for them American civilization was, essentially, not something new but an arm of Christian civilization extending into the new continent. Emma Willard, a pioneer in the education of women in the United States, wrote in the prefaces of her many texts of the "youthful simplicity" and "maiden purity" of America, but the texts made it clear that Americans were, first and foremost, Christians — by which she meant Protestants. For Willard, who did not engage in homespun-yeomen sociology, the only real difference between Americans and European Protestants was the special relationship that Americans had with Providence. By her account, Providence appeared time after time in the middle of battles to lead Americans on to victory. (Just where Providence went when they suffered defeat she did not say.) From a religious principle, Providence had grown into a force for nationalism. Willard and her contemporaries often spoke of "the New World," but it is clear that they meant only their part of it. For them, the real enemy was not the British or the French but the Papacy and the Catholic Spanish — specifically, those who had colonized the southern part of the American hemisphere. She and the other textbook writers of the period do not dwell on the American Revolution, because the tradition most important to them was established during the religious wars in Europe in the seventeenth century. And it is this imported European tradition that their textbooks make the centerpiece of America's national identity.

The assumption that all Americans were Protestants — and elected ones at that — remained in the textbooks until the eighteen-nineties, or until just about the time the public-high-school system became larger than the collection of church-based private schools. For the new generation of teachers, who were the servants of various bits of the state, the proper subject of American history was politics and the activities of government. The texts of the eighteen-nineties are silent on religious matters — gone is the violent anti-Catholicism, never to return — and highly articulate on the subject of the nation-state. From these texts, one might even imagine that the educators had come to take a completely secular view of society, in which "Americans" had no particular qualities but only their citizenship. This would be a mistake. The eighteen-nineties texts are merely impassive, and their impassivity conceals an important evolution taking place in the minds of the educators. The earlier nineteenth-century texts had defined the American identity by religion; the twentieth-century texts would define it by race and culture.

After 1900, a new distinction appears in American-history textbooks: there are "we Americans," and there are "the immigrants." The textbook discovery of "the immigrants" was actually somewhat belated, since the great wave of European immigration to the United States had been under way for some time. Europeans — and particularly Irish and Germans — had been crossing the Atlantic in large numbers since the eighteen-forties, but between 1881 and 1890 more than five million immigrants came to the United States, and by 1910 the total had risen to more than sixteen million. The newcomers not only increased the American population significantly but altered its ethnic composition. After 1900, immigrants from the southern and eastern countries of Europe vastly outnumbered those from the northern and western ones. The schools were particularly affected, since they were the only public agencies that offered special services for the immigrants. Having been charged with the "Americanization" of the newcomers, they naturally had to take on the task of defining what "an American" was and was not.

At this point, the texts began to emphasize the English ancestry of Americans. In their discussions of exploration and colonization, they gave far greater space and approval to Sir Francis Drake than to any of the other explorers except Columbus, and they concentrated on the English colonists to the near-exclusion of the French, the Spanish, and the Dutch. In contrast to both earlier and later books, they played down the motives of religious dissent and a desire to escape from a rigid class system and pointed up the purely commercial motive. They viewed the Colonies as extensions of England into the New World, and they looked on the American Revolution as a matter of practical politics more than anything else. The texts of the nineteenth century and those of the nineteen-thirties and after go on at length about the special virtues of Americans and the specialness of American culture and political institutions. The majority of the texts that were published between 1910 and 1930 are far less nationalistic; they emphasize continuity and evolution within a civilization. They also — as the Irish and German communities in Chicago pointed out — acclaim the American entry into the First World War on the side of the British.

That the textbook discovery of English roots coincided with the arrival of the new non-English immigrants may have been purely fortuitous. Nevertheless, these texts had a particular kind of perspective on the newcomers. Reasonably enough, they viewed the arrival of nine million people as a problem for the United States. Reasonably enough, they reported that the task of assimilation, or "Americanization," was one of the greatest strains ever put on American society. These were merely neutral observations. But the texts portrayed the immigrants as nothing more than a problem. Until the nineteen-thirties, they gave no information about how these people lived, what they did, or where they came from, much less why they came. Social history was not the strong point of those texts; still, they performed something of a feat in turning this vast new group of people into a total abstraction. "Can we assimilate and mold into citizenship the millions who are coming to our shores, or will they remain an ever-increasing body of aliens, an undigested and indigestible element in our body politic, and a constant menace to our free institutions?"[43] Such was a typical formulation of the problem for "us." The texts of the twenties expressed a good deal of pessimism about assimilation. Some of their worries were political. Apparently persuaded by the Red scare, the more conservative texts showed concern about "radical agitators" and "Bolsheviki" among the immigrants. According to the most popular of the texts, David Saville Muzzey's *American History*, these people were like rotten apples in a barrel — they had to be picked out and thrown back. Other texts found different groups of undesirables. One text, harking back to the theme of the wily Europeans, proposed that, while America had always been hospitable to honest folk, the European governments had on occasion abused this hospitality by using the country as "a dumping ground for convicts, paupers, anarchists and other undesirable citizens."[44]

Most of the twenties texts found virtue in the law establishing immigration quotas on the basis of the national origin of the American population in 1890. Those of a Progressive cast skirted the national-origins issue and justified the quotas on economic grounds. One, for instance, argued that there was no more space left in the country to put people — that any further influx would reduce all Americans to a "common level of misery." Another worried that the "great accumulation of wealth," on the one hand, and "the foreigners," on the other, would prevent the society from achieving its goal of economic security and a relative equality of wealth for all. This text then said cautiously, "Great racial groups, especially such as speak foreign languages, or belong to races with which we do not readily intermarry, do add to the difficulty of solving certain social problems." Most texts were less explicit on the issue of race, but a concern for it flickered through all the discussions of immigrants. For those texts that, like Muzzey, used "race" and "nationality" interchangeably, the immigrants clearly posed an intractable problem: if Americans were defined as belonging to the English race, then it was impossible to Americanize anyone who did not belong to it. The pessimism of these texts is quite understandable.

By about 1930, the texts had resolved this race-nationality confusion and become rather more optimistic about the prospects for Americanization. For Eugene C. Barker, William E. Dodd, and Henry Steele Commager, in *Our Nation's Development*, the question was: "Would it be possible to absorb the millions of olive-skinned Italians and swarthy black-haired Slavs and dark-eyed Hebrews into the body of the American people? Would they adjust themselves to their New World environment and understand and contribute to American institutions?" Their answer was yes, probably.[45] More liberal texts maintained that the European immigrants were already doing very well. According to Charles Garrett Vannest and Henry Lester Smith's *Socialized History of the United States*, the Jews were "conspicuously successful in the various forms of theatrical enterprise, and have been financially successful in most of the work they have undertaken." The Irish were doing well in politics, and the Germans were farming successfully; in fact, no one was causing any trouble except the Japanese and the Chinese, who "have brought a race problem to our Western states."[46] Harold Rugg's *An Introduction to Problems of American Culture*, one text in his series on American civilization, called for a new understanding between Americans and immigrants. The immigrants, it said, were contributing their manual labor, their Old World customs, and their fine arts to this country, and "we" ought to appreciate these things. The foreign-born, on the other hand, should learn to appreciate our ideals and should make a responsible effort to help realize them. In the thirties, the Rugg texts were among the few to call the United States "a melting pot."[47]

The notion that America was "a melting pot" entered the majority of the texts during the forties. In the forties and fifties, it was the catch phrase for all discussions of the immigrants, and the Statue of Liberty was the illustration beside them. These two symbols did not have wholly positive connotations in all texts, however. According to the 1955 edition of Muzzey, "America has been called the 'melting pot' because of these millions of people of foreign speech and customs who have been thrown in with our native colonial stock to be fused into a new type of American. Some students of society (sociologists) think that the process has injured our country by introducing a base alloy. Others point to the benefits which the brains and the hands of the immigrants have brought."[48] Instead of resolving this alleged controversy, the book proposes, "There is much to be said for each side of the question." The majority of the forties and fifties texts are much less equivocal; they are also rather more solipsistic. By their account, the immigrants are fine people, because their decision to come to the United States proves that this is a land of liberty; the fact that they were not turned away — by the Statue of Liberty — proves that Americans are uniquely generous. Then, in order to prove that American generosity has not been squandered, the texts list the "contributions" that individual immigrants have made to America.

In the mid-fifties, the texts commonly devoted several pages to pictures and short biographies of "immigrants," the conservative books selecting such figures as Andrew Carnegie, Lily Pons, and Augustus Saint-Gaudens, the more liberal ones choosing such as Serge Koussevitsky, Leopold Stokowski, Albert Einstein, and Irving Berlin.[49] Just why, apart from Carnegie, the texts emphasized artists and intellectuals is an interesting question. A cynic with the perspective of the seventies might conclude that artists and intellectuals were less threatening than other sorts of successful people. Still, it is a fact that the textbooks had traditionally associated art with immigrants. The Rugg books had pointed to fine arts as a foreign contribution, and back in the twenties another book had urged tolerance for the immigrants on the ground that many of them came from regions where there were ancient Greek and Roman ruins and "they all seemed to love painting, sculpture and music." What lay behind this association was, of course, the Websterian notion that all Americans were homespun yeomen and all Europeans either downtrodden peasants or effete, artistic aristocrats. And these books, being liberal, were trying to make the best of it. (As a consequence, there may be pockets of people in their forties who still believe that all people with complicated names must be artists.)

Interestingly enough, the textbook adoption of the melting-pot theory did not end the we-they distinction or really change the textbook notion of an American. The schoolbooks often spoke of an "amalgam," but besides artists, and people hanging off boats looking at the Statue of Liberty, they showed only people who looked like Anglo-Saxon Protestants. These people were ubiquitous in street scenes and military formations as well as in the President's Cabinet. The dominance of this particular species resulted from a strange reversal: in presuming an amalgam, the texts had once again begun to presume a homogeneous society — and thus to ignore the differences they had once so clearly seen.*

Only in the early sixties did most of the texts cease to talk about "the immigrants" as distinct from "us Americans." The coming of a new orthodoxy — "We are a nation of immigrants" — coincided, perhaps accidentally, with the first appearance of American art in the texts. It was not until the late sixties, however, that the texts began to picture Americans with other than Wasp faces and

* Moon, Cline, and MacGowan, *Story of Our Land and People* (1955), provides numerous examples of this: page 436 gives a black-and-white photograph of a mother and daughter watching a woman on television; page 451 shows a picture of customers at an early Woolworth's department store; page 599 shows a Norman Rockwell–style graphic of a family dinner-table scene.

names. And then the shattering of the single image of "an American" occurred not because of pressure from Irish-Americans, Italian-Americans, or Jews but because of the black civil-rights movement.

That the civil-rights movement should have been responsible for showing us the faces and real histories of immigrants from Southern and Eastern Europe is doubly ironic, because until the mid-sixties black Americans had hardly entered the textbooks at all. In the nineteen-thirties, the most progressive of social histories, the Rugg books, identified "the Negro" as a "social problem"; Rugg, as one might expect, counselled tolerance and an appreciation of the contributions made by such men as Booker T. Washington and Paul Robeson. The Rugg books were exceptional in this respect; few books published then or earlier noted the existence of blacks in contemporary America, and still fewer recorded the name of an individual. In the vast majority of books, there were only "the slaves"—slaves who had appeared magically in this country at some unspecified time and had disappeared with the end of the Civil War. The books of the thirties were less inclined to racist characterizations than their predecessors, but they were wholly complacent about the welfare and happiness of the slaves.* Not until the late forties did the majority of the books follow Rugg's lead and show free black people. The books of the forties and fifties tended to speak condescendingly of the progress that "the Negro" had made

* Barker, Dodd, and Commager, *Our Nation's Development* (1937), page 269, reads, for example, "Nor was the slave always unhappy in his cabin. On the contrary, he sang at his work. . . . If his cabin was small, there were shade trees about it, a vegetable garden near by and chickens in his coop. . . . On this fare . . . the slaves multiplied as fast as the white people."

in educating "himself," and to include a picture of Booker T. Washington or Jackie Robinson.[50] The Muzzey text of the period, however, began its first section on the population of the United States by saying, "Leaving aside the Negro and Indian population," and it proceeded to do just that.[51] The blacks were never treated as a group at all; they were quite literally invisible.

In the mid-sixties came a period, still embarrassing to the publishers, when the texts took a sudden and overwhelming interest in peanuts and the United Nations Secretariat — or so one might conclude, given the multiple appearances of George Washington Carver and Ralph Bunche. These black instant celebrities seemed to have come from another country or another planet, since there was otherwise no mention of blacks in America. Shortly afterward, black faces appeared as if by magic in the same photographs and cartoons that had had only white faces before — the marks of drypointing almost visible. Then sections on the civil-rights movement turned up in the very backs of the books — as it were, in the back of the bus. But this period of tokenism did not last very long, for in addition to outside pressures there was — in the history texts, at least — the problem of internal consistency: either the blacks belonged to American history or they did not, and if they did they belonged to all of it. To include a section on the civil-rights movement meant that the whole of American history had to be rewritten to include blacks and their perspective on events. It was as if Tolstoy had first written *War and Peace* without the character of Pierre.

By the early seventies, most of the books had been rewritten to include the history of blacks in America. All those published for a national audience record the history of the civil-rights movement in its proper place. In the indexes of many of the books of the early seventies, there are entries under "Blacks" for the Colonial period, the American Revolution, the Spanish-American War, the Truman Administration, and so on, as well as for those periods when racial issues dominated white American politics. All at least mention Frederick Douglass and Martin Luther King, Jr., and some have extensive discussions of their work; in these texts, Booker T. Washington never walks without W. E. B. Du Bois. Some of the books are more politically adventurous than others: some discuss Malcolm X, Huey Newton, and Nat Turner, while others huddle around Sojourner Truth and the N.A.A.C.P. But in all the books a certain prescribed percentage of black faces appears in photographs showing assembly lines, military formations, and mayoral conferences. In the main, this rewriting of history involved no profound alteration: it was merely a matter of adding, of putting in what was not there before. But in the history of one period the addition of a black perspective implied, and necessarily brought, a complete change. That period was Reconstruction. Of all the events that were rewritten in the mid-sixties, Reconstruction was revised the most dramatically. To compare the books of the mid-sixties with those of the early seventies on this subject is to see not a change of emphasis but a total inversion: the same material is used, nothing has been added, but the interpretation has altered so that — one might say — what was white is now black and vice versa.

The version of Reconstruction that most Americans who are now adults grew up with included a more or less passionate defense of President Andrew Jackson in his struggle with the Radical Republicans. The texts published from the beginning of the century to the mid-sixties were unanimous in their view that Johnson should never have been impeached. Though the President was temperamentally unsuited to his job, they argued, his program for Reconstruction was good, because, among other things, it offered amnesty to the former Confederates as individuals. The Radical Republicans — including "the harsh, vindictive" Thaddeus Stevens — voted to impeach and convict mainly because they wanted revenge on the South and a permanent electoral majority. According to these books, Radical Reconstruction was an unmitigated disaster. The Reconstruction governments were imposed on the South with federal bayonets and were run by a lot of unscrupulous "carpetbaggers" and "scalawags." Instead of reconstructing the region, they pillaged it. The legislatures — filled with ignorant Negroes who obeyed the dictates of the carpetbaggers and scalawags — engaged in an "orgy of spending." The legislators embezzled funds and voted themselves huge gold watches, imported perfume, and champagne. The tremendous corruption of these governments, combined with the anarchy caused by bands of Negroes roaming the countryside, finally forced the Southerners to take action. The use of violence by the Southerners was deplorable, but the Northerners could not have expected the Southerners to submit to Negro rule, and the Ku Klux Klan had a worse reputation than it deserved. In the beginning, the Klan was an organization of respectable white Southerners who banded together in their own self-defense. True, it was eventually taken over by lawless men with selfish interests, but shortly afterward it was forced to disband, mainly because the solid citizens of the region disapproved of it.[52] The texts published before the late sixties differed on certain matters of tactics. Not all of them in any given period favored the Black Codes — the laws, passed by the defeated states before the Radical Reconstruction, that, among other things, required blacks to carry evidence of employment. From the thirties on, the texts tended to disagree about whether the Freedmen's Bureau actually helped the former slaves or merely gave them the ridiculous illusion that they were owed forty acres and a mule. Some texts from this period mentioned the existence of the Jim Crow laws. All of them, however, stated firmly that, with or without these laws, the situation in the South improved only when Reconstruction ended and "the Southerners" regained control of their governments.

One remarkable thing about this version of events was that it appeared in texts designed for Northern schools; however, these texts did not have the white Southerners' perspective on the Civil War—only on Reconstruction. Another interesting thing was that this version of Reconstruction came into the Northern texts between 1900 and 1910. Until around 1900, the Northern texts had treated the South almost as a foreign country: the Confederacy was "the slave power," and the war "the great rebellion." Johnson was an obnoxious figure to them, and to the extent that they considered the plight of the white Southerners at all they judged that the rebels had got only what was coming to them. But then such staunch New Englanders as David Saville Muzzey and such left-wing Progressives as Willis Mason West had adopted the perspective of the Southern aristocrats. The intellectual heirs of Charles Sumner and Henry Adams gushed sentimentally about the decline of the great plantations and the trials of Southern womanhood. The speed of this change in perspective was astonishing. But it was matched by the one that took place in the nineteen-sixties.

The current version of events—and the truth of the matter for those under twenty-five—is that Reconstruction was not a bad thing at all. According to the seventies texts, Andrew Johnson was the wrong man for the Presidency after the war: he lacked dignity and judgment, and concern for the rights of the freedmen. The Radical Republicans — including "the courageous Thaddeus Stevens" — had two excellent reasons for opposing Johnson's plan to allow the Southern states back into the Union: first, the state governments had passed the Black Codes and thus all but reëstablished slavery; second, by failing to accord blacks the vote they had all but insured that those who lost the war would end up controlling the United States Congress. Whether or not Johnson deserved impeachment, the Radicals brought a necessary reform to the South by permitting blacks to vote and also giving poor whites a chance to participate in their own governments. The Reconstruction state legislatures were dominated not by former slaves (only in South Carolina did the blacks have a majority, and there in the lower house alone) but by people the white Southerners called carpetbaggers and scalawags, some of whom were adventurers but many of whom were sincere reformers. Corruption existed in these governments, but it existed in the South both before and after Reconstruction, and it was just as prevalent in the North during that period. Public spending was enormous mainly because there was so much to be done to help the freedmen and to rebuild the devastated economy of the South. White Southerners formed a number of secret societies to oppose the Reconstruction governments, one of which was the Ku Klux Klan. To prevent the freedmen from voting, the Klan waged a campaign of terror against the blacks which included arson, beatings, and murder. Reconstruction ended, in 1877, as a result of a secret deal between Republican leaders and Southern businessmen. That deal may have saved the Union, but it robbed the blacks of the vote and put them at a serious political and economic disadvantage for nearly a century.[53]

The textbook treatment of Reconstruction offers the most striking example of the gap between the academic world and the secondary schools. The first version of Reconstruction derived from the work of Professor William A. Dunning and the so-called Dunning school of historiography, founded in the eighteen-nineties. In the early thirties, that school was successfully challenged by Francis Simkins and other historians. These progressive historians argued from the assumption that the fate of the blacks was just as important as the fate of the whites in the South. In analyzing the end of Reconstruction, they looked to the identity of interests between the Northern industrialists and the upper-class white Southerners. In academic circles, their version of Reconstruction became the dominant one by the end of the thirties. But it took thirty years and the civil-rights movement to put it into the high-school texts. In the fifties, Kenneth Stampp and oher historians added to this revisionist thesis by arguing the virtues of the Radical Republican position — and their work, too, is reflected in recent texts. In the sixties, Staughton Lynd and certain New Left historians came up with the striking new thesis that the Radical Republicans had not gone far enough, and that their failure to deliver on their promises to give the free slaves economic independence doomed the blacks to inferior status and the country to racial conflict for generations to come.[54] The current texts do not even suggest this interpretation as a possibility.

Textbook wisdom would, of course, suggest that racist attitudes become more pronounced the further back one goes in history; or, to put it another way, that white Americans have grown slowly but steadily toward enlightenment during the last two hundred years. But this is not true even with respect to the texts themselves. The texts do show a slow but constant movement toward the acceptance of non-Anglo-Saxon immigrants, and they show a sudden, revolutionary change in attitude toward black Americans, but with regard to the American Indians they show a different pattern entirely. In this regard, their progress toward enlightenment is, if anything, resolutely backward over the course of a century.

In the texts of the eighteen-thirties and eighteen-forties, the North American Indians are presented as interesting, important people — in spite of the fact that they are not Christians. Emma Willard and her contemporaries describe the characteristics of the various tribal groups and discuss individual leaders at some length. In an age still innocent of anthropology, they give a remarkable amount of attention to the customs, the tools, and the probable origins of the "native Americans." There are, of course, some lapses from science. One writer, for instance, speculates that the Indians might have climbed up a root from the center of the earth (a native American legend). But then he quickly turns around and proposes what was the conventional textbook wisdom of the period — that they had walked across "the Behering Strait" from Asia sometime after the Flood. These writers have a few negative things to say about the Indians — they accuse the "aborigines" of treating their women cruelly and making war without declaring it — but on the whole their characterizations are rather favorable. According to the Reverend Charles A. Goodrich, the Indians are "quick of apprehension, and not wanting in genius . . . friendly . . . distinguished for gravity and eloquence [and] bravery."[55] For these writers, it goes without saying that civilized people have a (God-given) right to the continent. But it is their opinion that "we Americans" have treated the Indians rather badly, and their strong recommendation is that in the future we make efforts to civilize them and convert them to Christianity.

This rather high level of concern for the Indians began to decline in the texts of the eighteen-forties and diminished progressively as the century wore on. The post–Civil War writers not only gave the Indians less space but had apparently forgotten a lot of what their predecessors knew about them. Ignorant now of ethnography, they referred to the Indian nations as "savage," "barbarous," and "half-civilized," and left it at that. As time went on, their characterizations of Indian culture became more and more negative. To the writers of the eighteen-nineties, the Indians had a few admirable traits, such as bravery, endurance, keen observation, and a sense of hospitality, but these were far outweighed by bad qualities: they were treacherous, cruel, tyrannical to women, idolatrous, lazy, vengeful, and given to torture. The pre–Civil War writers had described the Indians idiosyncratically; they differed, for instance, on how talkative or untalkative the Indians were. Their successors were not so original. In the eighteen-nineties, the characterization of the Indians crystallized into a precise and unvarying formula, which, once set, did not change for thirty years. The texts of the nineteen-twenties, like those of the eighteen-nineties, portrayed the Indians as lazy, childlike, and cruel. Those few writers who expanded on the formula drew from literature rather than from life. For Muzzey, the Indians were "now immovable as a rock, now capricious as the April breeze";

another writer quoted Longfellow's "Hiawatha."[56] Not until the nineteen-thirties was this formula abandoned—and then only because the whole subject was dropped.

The progressive decline of textbook concern for the Indians is easy to understand if one remembers that nineteenth-century text writers came from the East. In the first half of the century, Indians were a physical presence in the East. Moreover, they were a distinguishing mark of the new continent—something that the Old World could not claim for itself. As such, they were an object of national pride: they may have been savages, but they were our savages. Then, as the century wore on and the Indians were forced to move to the West, they became more and more marginal to the concerns of the nation. The text writers naturally grew indifferent to them. But that the writers should at the same time have grown hostile is less understandable. Practical considerations certainly do not explain the hostility, since early in the century the Indians posed a real threat to the settlers and in the eighteen-nineties they did not: the frontier was closed, and the tribes had been exterminated or confined to reservations. The Indians were no longer enemies of the Americans—they were their victims. But perhaps that is just the point: not battles for survival but massacres must have justification by evil.

By the nineteen-thirties, the American memory, incarnate in the history texts, had blocked out both the Indians and their fate. In the nineteen-thirties, the only texts that even mentioned the Indians were those for lower grades, whose authors clearly intended to interest children with tales of a colorful, exotic people who behaved, as one book put it bluntly, just like children. Their Indians were cigar-store and movie Indians. Then, in the forties and fifties, even this image faded out. One best-selling text of the period had when it was first published, in 1931, a long description of Indians at play, Indians trading, Indians worshipping the spirits. By the 1942 edition, these pages had collapsed into a few paragraphs, of which the last is headed "The Indians Were Backward"; by the 1950 edition, even this paragraph had gone. The Indians, it appeared, were too frivolous a subject for children growing up into "the great struggle for freedom."* It was not until the mid-sixties that the texts took up the subject of the Indians again. They did not say very much about the Indians themselves but did describe the terrible destruction wreaked upon them in the eighteen-seventies and the unhappy results of United States government policy concerning them in the twentieth century. The Indians, in other words, had become a function of the Vietnam War. Only in the early seventies, and as a direct result of agitation for Indian rights, did the Indians become something (though not much) more than the objects of official American policy.

The textbooks made many discoveries about Americans during the nineteen-sixties. The country they had conceived as male and Anglo-Saxon turned out to be filled with blacks, "ethnics," Indians, Asians, and women. (The history texts have not actually found many women in America, but they have replaced their pictures of Dolley Madison with photographs of Susan B. Anthony.) The country also turned out to be filled with Spanish-speaking

* For example, the Casner and Gabriel textbooks over this period evidence a decline in interest in the American Indians in terms of the number of pages which make reference to the Indians: in *The Rise of American Democracy* (1938), the index shows 76 pages under the general heading; *The Story of American Democracy* (1942), the index shows 45 pages; and *The Story of American Democracy* (1950) shows only 25 pages.

people who had come from Mexico, Puerto Rico, and other countries of the Caribbean basin. This last of their discoveries was — at least, to judge from the space they gave it — the most important one next to the discovery of the blacks. In books of the early seventies, there were two- and four-page color spreads on Puerto Rico and on "The Mexican Heritage" and "Mexican Americans Today," these featuring pictures of Toltec statues, César Chávez, and Anthony Quinn. The sudden eruption of Latinos was, of course, the publishers' response to pressure from the powerful school boards of Texas, California, and New York — states that harbored a great percentage of the new immigrants from the south. The pressures were apparently unexpected, for the photographs of César Chávez and the Toltec statues stand out as uncomfortably in these books as the photographs of George Washington Carver and the civil-rights marches do in the books of the mid-sixties. There is little actual history behind them. The previous editions of these texts had contained some history of Latin America, but it had had to be cut, because of its condescending tone.

The textbook tradition, in fact, served the newest immigrant population rather worse than it served any other group. In the first place, the Spanish colonizers of the New World had always been American history's villains par excellence. In the early nineteenth century, the Reverend Jedidiah Morse had devoted heartfelt efforts to a defamation of the Spanish character. This was just a start; his successors throughout the nineteenth century reserved their most vitriolic prose for the Spanish and their doings, going on at great length about gold lust, cruelty to Indians, and crazed searchings for the Fountain of Youth. The sturdy tradition of Hispanophobia continued undiluted until the nineteen-twenties. At that point, a small minority of texts began to make concessions. The Spanish, these texts said, lacked "moral and ethical character," but they had made certain contributions to the New World; they had, after all, discovered it, and they had brought it Christianity, mission architecture, and domestic animals.[57] As time went on, this "balanced" approach gradually took over the books, and by the nineteen-thirties it was the conventional wisdom; it continued as such until the late sixties. The tone, however, remained distinctly jaundiced. One book that was published in 1967 and is still in use in some schools summarizes the whole subject of the Spanish colonization in two short sections entitled "Spain Monopolizes Much of the World" and "Spain Makes Many Contributions But Permits Few Freedoms." In this very capitalistic and Cold War book, the word "monopoly" is as much anathema as "effeminacy" or "luxury" was in the Reverend Mr. Morse's text, and the permission of "few freedoms" is the moral equivalent of papism. The typical text of the late sixties and early seventies takes a slightly less dogmatic attitude. A good example is to be found in the 1973 revised printing of an older text, *The Adventure of the American People*, by Henry F. Graff and John A. Krout. The text makes some effort to describe Spanish feudalism as a system and goes on to list the "contributions" of the Spanish — most of which are crops. The Spanish section concludes:

> Although we can see after four hundred years what things were of enduring significance in the Spanish settlements, at the time only gold seemed worthwhile. In fact, the Spanish conquerors never took on the tasks of taming the forests and rivers of America and colonizing the land.

Finding gold so easily and so early drove them madly on to look for more. They never found it, but the search left its mark on Spanish culture in the New World, and in its turn it also affected the mother country. . . .

At home, the Spaniards failed to reinvest the gold and silver drawn from the mines of the New World. When they had used it up, Spain lived only on memories of its past. Gambling always on "hitting the jackpot," it left to others the richest prize of all — what later became the United States. How different our history might have been if our own abundant gold and silver deposits had been found first by the Spaniards![58]

A number of the mid-seventies books have broken the tradition of two centuries by making no reference to gold, slavery, or massacres of Indians in connection with the Spanish. (The principle that lies behind textbook history is that the inclusion of nasty information constitutes bias even if the information is true.) But this bowdlerization has not really brought the books any closer to the truth, for the real distortion of the texts lay less in what they said about the Spanish than in what they did not say. The students of Graff and Krout might be shocked to learn, as they could from Howard Mumford Jones, in *O Strange New World*, that while the "forlorn little band of Englishmen were trying to stick it out on Roanoke Island three hundred poets were competing for a prize in Mexico City," and that when Jefferson was President the great scientist Alexander von Humboldt declared that, of all the cities in the Western Hemisphere, Mexico City had the most solid scientific institutions.[59]

That textbook historians detested the Spanish colonizers did not mean that they therefore sympathized with the colonized peoples. The same writers who were eloquent on the subject of Spanish gold lust also tended to revel in the gory details of Aztec human sacrifices. Montezuma, it seemed, deserved Cortés. About the other native peoples of the region the texts said little or nothing. And when they dropped the Spanish they dropped the whole history of Latin America. In 1848, "the Mexicans" would crop up in the context of a border war; in 1898, "the Cubans" and "the Puerto Ricans" would make an appearance as the grateful beneficiaries of the Spanish-American War. Who these people were remained mysterious, for the texts, whether or not they justified these wars per se, never credited the Mexicans or the Cubans with having any views. The Latin-American nations were, it appeared, nothing more than the objects of United States foreign policy.[60]

Having cut out most of these offending passages, the text publishers may now be on the verge of rewriting history backward to accommodate the new population of Spanish-speaking Americans. If so, the histories of the future will be interesting to see, for the rewriting will affect not only domestic social history but the whole textbook notion of the space that the United States has occupied in the New World.

Only in the nineteen-sixties did the textbooks finally end their rear-guard action on behalf of a Northern European America. The civil-rights movement had shattered the image of a homogeneous American society and, for the first time in the twentieth century, raised profound questions about the national identity. The answer given by that movement and accepted as orthodoxy by most state and big-city school boards was that the United States is a multiracial, multicultural society. This formula, however, raised as many questions as it answered. Was the United States really like Yugoslavia — a country held together only by a delicate balance among ethnic and cultural groups? Or was there some integration of these groups? Was there a dominant culture — and was that a good thing? Was there some principle of unity that Americans ought to support apart from that of the state? The current texts show signs of struggle with these questions. The struggle has had no clear outcome, for the social portrait drawn by the texts remains divided and confused.

The current texts represent the United States as a multiracial society to the extent that they include some material on all the large racial and ethnic groups, and that their photographs show people of all colors (also of all ages and both sexes) and suggest that even white Americans come from different ethnic backgrounds. The books contain a good deal of social history on these groups. Most texts assert that the early settlers had African as well as European roots, and virtually all of them have sections on Aztec, Mayan, and North American Indian cultures. In one text, the account of colonization begins with the settlement of Puerto Rico by Ponce de León. Another text begins with a chapter on immigrants and includes a discussion of the migration of blacks from South to North after the Second World War. The texts also describe certain of the "problems" that minorities have faced in the United States, such as the internment of Japanese-Americans during the Second World War.[61] But it's on the subject of these "problems" that the texts are still confused. They have succeeded in including all groups, but they have not succeeded in treating them all equally. There is, for instance, a remarkable disparity between their treatment of

European ethnic groups and their treatment of all other ethnic minorities.

Most current texts discuss the European ethnic groups in two separate places — in their chapters on immigration and industrialization in the nineteenth century, and again in their chapters on modern-day life. Their nineteenth-century social history now includes a good deal of material that would have been labelled "too controversial" a decade ago. In place of the brief dismissive passages about toiling masses arriving in the land of liberty, the texts now describe in some painful detail the difficulties so many of the immigrants faced when they got off the boats: brutalizing labor in factories and mines, slum conditions in the cities, prejudice against them, and the shock of entering another culture. The so-called "inquiry," or "discovery," texts — which focus on a few topics and illustrate them with documents from primary and secondary sources — include portions of diaries or books by the newly arrived Europeans which present the experience from a perspective that was heretofore unthinkable: that of the immigrants themselves. In the sections on modern-day life, the texts make some attempt at consistency with this point of view. They describe not individual artists but working-class families that came originally from Poland, Greece, or Russia, and they contend that the European culture of these families has not melted away — that they still have strong religious, culinary, and other traditions. But here the discussion ends. With two exceptions, they do not discuss the assimilation of European ethnic groups; they do not discuss the washout of European traditions in America or the fusion of various cultures. They insist — following Nathan Glazer and Daniel P. Moynihan's sociological study

Beyond the Melting Pot[62] — that the "ethnics" have not been assimilated but have separately added to the wonderful variety of life in America. There is some irony in this. The very fact that the texts can depict the horrors of life for the immigrants in the eighteen-eighties shows that some assimilation has occurred; otherwise, the texts would be accused of offending group sensibilities. A further proof is that a number of the authors of these American-history books are the children or grandchildren of such immigrants.

Still, even with this overstatement of the Glazer-Moynihan thesis, the treatment of European minorities is far more realistic than that of non-European minorities, whose sensibilities the publishers are anxious not to offend. The photographs in the mass-market texts rarely show a non-white person who is brutalized, dirty, or even poor — unless the photograph specifically illustrates "pockets of poverty in America."[63] There are almost no pictures of black sharecroppers, or black laborers of any kind unless they are in integrated groups wearing hard hats. Except for Stokely Carmichael, other black militants, and the hardhat laborers, blacks pictured in current texts wear business suits or lab coats. The same goes for other non-white people. Most of them are smiling. You can find pictures of Chicano farmworkers, but the workers are always clean and look as if they're enjoying their work. They're always smiling at César Chávez. The Puerto Ricans are smiling and healthy. The Chinese are smiling at healthy-looking vegetable stands. Indeed, everyone is smiling so hard you would think that all non-white people in the United States took happy pills. (The Russians, by contrast, appear to be a sombre lot. Their grimness dates from a time in the fifties when a group of right-wing organizations made an enormous fuss about a photograph of smiling Russian children.) There are a few exceptions to this rule. But there are no exceptions to the rule of art. Many of the current texts overflow with examples of art by non-white people. In the first chapters, there are pages on which the printed word makes a few ant trails around huge color pictures of folk art: Mayan temples or Aztec masks, Iroquois blankets, Pueblo pottery (but no feather headdresses, for these are thought to be stereotypical). Later on, there are pictures of modern Mexican murals and disquisitions on black painters and writers, and occasionally on one or two black musicians. (One book includes a half-page reproduction of a painting in Hudson River school style that happens to have been painted by a black.) Apparently the publishers have yet to find a Puerto Rican landscape painter or a Chinese-American poet, but one imagines that they are trying hard, since artists must now come from everywhere except Europe. In addition to artists, the non-white minorities seem to have hero figures and "leaders," while the European groups do not; and all of them are always said to be struggling to achieve full rights.

The publishers have mentioned the struggles of non-white peoples, but in order to sell books to a majority they sometimes refrain from mentioning what these groups are struggling against. Though most books delineate the social and economic institutions that made life so hard for the nineteenth-century immigrants, they do not always do the same for the non-white Americans in modern times. The Chicano farmworkers are struggling, but some texts fail to mention the growers. The American Indians are struggling in a void, there being no mention of the historical arrangements between private corporations and the Bureau of Indian Affairs for the exploitation of natural resources on the tribal lands. In regard to the civil-rights movement, there is often no discussion of institutionalized racism — not even that which was contained in the Southern school systems before Little Rock. The books report at length on reform movements and reform measures but rarely tot up the results, thus giving little or no indication that many of the attempts at reform have failed. This is hardly surprising, since they usually fail to explain in any detail how or why the injustices came into being in the first place. As one critic has pointed out, the texts report that blacks fought in the Revolutionary War but not that the Framers of the Constitution, with the three-fifths compromise, among other provisions, made slavery a part of the political system. Furthermore, only the most sophisticated of the inquiry books report any of the "struggles to achieve full rights" from the point of view of the strugglers.

The current version of the history of racial minorities in America represents the compromise that the publishers have made among the conflicting demands of a variety of pressure groups, inside and outside the school systems. The compromise is an unhappy one, and it is bound to change in the future, if only because its inconsistencies are so obvious. However, it is interesting to ask at this point what a truly "multiracial, multicultural" history text would look like. The question is an academic one, admittedly, but there are certain organizations, such as the Council on Interracial Books for Children, that do argue it, in an academic way, and that do give certain answers through their criticisms of current texts. To look at the council's very detailed and sophisticated criticism of the texts is to see that somewhere — far from where the texts are now — there is a real dilemma in the very notion of a "multiracial, multicultural" history. Let us take an example. In its list of twenty-six "stereotypes, distortions and omissions" that the history texts generally make about "native Americans," the council points to a passage from one of the more naïve of the texts — *America: Its People and Values*, by Leonard C. Wood, Ralph H. Gabriel, and Edward L. Biller. The passage reads:

> A friendly Indian named Squanto helped the colonists. He showed them how to plant corn and how to live on the edge of the wilderness. A soldier, Captain Miles Standish, taught the Pilgrims how to defend themselves against unfriendly Indians.

The council's objection to this passage is that it is Eurocentric to characterize native Americans as either "friendly" or "unfriendly." Squanto was actually assisting invaders, whereas the "unfriendly" Indians were defending their communities. "All nations define a 'patriot' as one whose allegiance is toward his or her own people," the council report continues. "Consequently, true Native American heroes are those who fought to preserve and protect their people's freedom and land."[64]

The implications of that objection are far-reaching. To begin with, if the texts were really to consider American history from the perspective of the American Indians, they would have to conclude that the continent had passed through almost five hundred years of unmitigated disaster, beginning with the epidemics spread by the Europeans and continuing on most fronts today. Then, if the texts were really to consider the Indian point of view, they could not simply say this but would have to take the position of Squanto — if not that of his more patriotic fellows — and categorize Miles Standish as friendly or unfriendly. And ditto for the next four hundred years — while making sure, of course, to portray the diverse views of all the Indian nations, and their diverse relations with the white settlers. When you add to this, as the council would, the Chicano, Asian-American, African-American, Puerto Rican, and women's perspectives on events, American history becomes unbelievably complicated — as does the whole issue of what constitutes balance and fairness. But the inclusion of other perspectives is crucial to a multiracial or multiethnic history. Add to that the notion "multicultural" and there is yet another level of complexity involved, for culture, of course, is not the same as race, and (to raise a problem that neither the text writers nor their critics seem to have considered) some of the greatest cultural differences in the United States lie between Anglo-Saxon Protestant males. Conceivably, the publishers could make a book that would include all these perspectives — or, more realistically, they could produce different texts for the different sections of society. But in either case the message of the texts would be that Americans have no common history, no common culture, and no common values, and that membership in a racial or cultural group constitutes the most fundamental experience of each individual. The message would be that the center cannot, and should not, hold.

The logical extreme of the "multiracial, multicultural" position is worth considering, if only because it clarifies the traditional ideology of the texts. At least since the eighteen-nineties, the school histories have focussed more or less narrowly on the development of the nation-state. To the extent that they dealt with social history, they have assumed a fairly homogeneous society, in which all differences could be justly compromised to suit all parties. In practice, this has meant taking the position of the ruling groups — whoever they happened to be at any given time

— and suppressing the views of others. Since the nineteen-thirties, text writers have been lecturing children on the need for tolerance and respect for differences, but they have at the same time continued to minimize social conflicts and emphasize the similarities between Americans. The conflicts of the nineteen-sixties jolted only a small percentage of the texts out of this approach. The inquiry books, for extremely literate — and thus largely white, upper-middle-class — children, present cultural diversity and social conflict. The mass-market texts, for the less literate, picture people with "foreign-sounding" names and different-colored skin, but the message remains the traditional one: Americans are all alike, no matter what their color or their background.

The textbook doctrine of American homogeneity is nowhere more insistently stated than in the reporting of economics in American life. American-history texts are remarkable for their lack of economic analysis. In this most economically successful of societies, a child can hardly discover what a corporation is, to say nothing of the nature of the economy. And it has always been that way. The nineteenth-century writers paid no attention to economics at all; their interest lay in earthquakes, wars, and Presidents. It was only in the eighteen-nineties that the texts introduced the subject — and then only to boast of technological progress and the increasing wealth of the nation as a whole. The twentieth-century writers could not maintain the embargo — they had to discuss business, labor, the farmers, and so on — but, with few exceptions (and these mostly in the thirties, in the wake of economic disaster), they have been as squeamish about the subject of money as about the subjects of religion and sex.

The tone for twentieth-century writing on economics seems to have been set by the Mugwump writers, who dominated the text market for twenty years of the century (much longer in the case of Muzzey). The Mugwumps not only disliked the economic-interest groups — business was corrupt and labor full of subversives — but thought that there was something unnatural about them. To read their texts is to imagine that economics began with the Industrial Revolution and would disappear soon if all went well. (Muzzey's great period of pessimism occurred in the twenties and thirties, when he found that, far from disappearing, economic issues had become dominant concerns.) Addressing themselves to middle-class children, they noted briefly the inequities of the society and urged reform through the heightening of moral consciousness. The social norm they held out to children was a Jeffersonian vision of independent — and independently wealthy — citizens with a rough equality of political power and with the common good at heart. Industrialization was a reality they did not wish to deal with.[65]

This notion of moral salvation for American capitalism also inhabits the work of the more left-wing writers of the period, such as Willis Mason West. This is curious, for West, in his *American History and Government*, came as close as any text writer has ever done to making a class-conflict model of American history. In that work, which appeared in 1913, he discussed, for instance, the American Revolution as a social upheaval as well as a war for independence, and spoke of the "warlike" relation between labor and capital at the beginning of the century. He faced the fact that in the last half of the nineteenth century "great multitudes were worse off than any considerable portion of society in earlier times," and concluded, "The modern industrial organization *produces* wealth with gratifying rapidity, but it fails to *distribute* wealth properly." The solution he suggested, however, had to do with conscience, not with institutional reorganization.[66]

The textbook that best describes economic conflicts in America remains the 1923 edition of Charles and Mary Beard's *History of the United States.* The Beards, almost alone among text writers, described the relationship between politics and economics in the nineteenth century. For instance, their text says, "The outcome of the Civil War in the South was nothing short of a revolution. The ruling class, the law, and the government of the old order had been subverted." And later it says, "The corporation, in fact, became the striking feature of American business life, one of the most marvelous institutions of all time, comparable in wealth and power and the number of its servants with kingdoms and states of old."[67] This is to give the Industrial Revolution the drama it deserves — and to convey the real truth of the matter. The texts never achieved this level of veracity again — in part, simply because their rhetoric lacked this force of self-confidence. (Compare the language of one recent text, *United States History: Search for Freedom,* by Richard N. Current, Alexander DeConde, and Harris L. Dante: "After the war, the governments of the southern states went through a bewildering series of changes," and "The Industrial Revolution and the accompanying agricultural revolution had far-reaching consequences.")[68] However, the Beard book is short on the economic analysis of the Constitution for which Charles Beard, in his *Economic Interpretation of the Constitution,* was well known. Similarly, West's discussion of the American Revolution as a social upheaval did not appear in his subsequent texts. Apparently, even the most liberal audiences held the Revolution and the Constitutional period to be sacred ground for children.

The liberal texts of the nineteen-thirties made much the same critique of the economy as their Mugwump predecessors. Pointing always to a norm of relative equality of wealth between citizens, they promised that this condition could be achieved without drastic institutional change. Harold Rugg, one of the most left-wing of the writers, asserted that although the national income was large enough to provide everyone with a high standard of living, one-tenth of the population received a third of that income and the mass of people had barely enough to live on. Rugg attributed unemployment to laborsaving machinery and the lack of planning; he insisted that with government planning — though not government ownership of industry — poverty could be eliminated. Like his Mugwump predecessors, Rugg did not analyze the changes in the economy over time or relate these changes to politics; along with most of his contemporaries, he treated economics as merely a "problem" in the present. What was most original about his economic analysis was his description of how various representative families in the United States lived. In his *Introduction to Problems of American Culture*, he contrasted the lives of Mr. Very Poor Man, Mr. Average Worker, Mr. Average White Collar Man, Mr. Prosperous Businessman, and Mr. Cultured Man. His clear identification with Mr. Cultured Man, who to some extent defied economic categorization, did not prevent the portraits from revealing quite a lot about the economic system. Certainly they showed the economic inequalities of American society (the black population excepted) far better than mere statistics on income distribution could.

Such social realism in the texts was brought to an end

in the early nineteen-forties, by the nationwide attack, sponsored by the National Association of Manufacturers, on Rugg's series of texts on American civilization for elementary and junior high school. Few of the textbooks of the forties, fifties, or early sixties gave any current income-distribution figures or admitted the existence of any form of inequality — economic, political, legal, or other. The books were as purely boosterish in their description of "the American way of life" as a Radio Free Europe broadcast. But there was an irony in their description — an irony symbolized by the fact that they almost never used the word "capitalism." The books went on and on about the glories of free enterprise — they were far more enthusiastic about it than about the Bill of Rights — but they never actually explained how the American economy worked, or how it had changed over time. Conceivably, the authors feared that it was not really a free-enterprise system — or perhaps they thought that any precise description of it (even the word "capitalism") would imply the existence of alternatives. Some of the fifties texts, such as Henry W. Bragdon and Samuel P. McCutchen's *History of a Free People*, did an excellent job of describing such epiphenomena as the free-silver movement and the Hawley-Smoot tariff, but that was the end of their economic analysis. The children of the fifties thus remained wholly ignorant of the virtues as well as the vices of their own economic system.

In the current texts, this ban on economic history remains largely in force. The one exception is the period of industrialization in the latter part of the nineteenth century. Most books now not only describe the technical achievements of the period but explain the notion of capital formation, outline the philosophy of the "captains of industry," and give some account of the revolutionary changes that industrialism made in American society. Through photographs more than in words, they manage to conjure up the huge creative energies and equally huge destructiveness of early American capitalism. The rest of their economics reporting is dull and uninformative. They talk vaguely about agricultural development in the first half of the nineteenth century but fail to mention the land speculation that provided the motor for so much of the Westward movement. They are fairly good on the early dramas of unionization but uninformative on twentieth-century labor-union history. They report on the economic and social legislation of the Progressive period and the New Deal, but almost all of them fail to describe the essential transformation of American capitalism in the twentieth century. As far as these histories are concerned, the United States still has a free-market economy that runs by national supply and demand, with government providing certain regulatory and social services. There is not even the most general description of the modern corporation, modern financial institutions, agribusiness, international trade and monetary agreements, or the tax structure. There is a near-ban on the terms "conglomerate" and "multinational corporation"; the word "corporation" tends to come up only in the context of the environmental movement — which is surely to put the cart before the horse. There is no analysis of the growth of service industries or the growth of the governmental sector. And, finally, there is no discussion of the relationship of economics to political power and the way people live.

What is most mysterious in the current texts is their treatment of social and economic inequality. It is not that the texts still present the society as a wall-to-wall middle-class suburbia. In the late sixties, all of them discovered a group that had presumably been extinct since the nineteen-thirties: the poor. Current texts depict the poor as having existed in three periods of American history — the Industrial Revolution, the Great Depression, and now. In their "America Today" sections, they have pictures of the poor — typically a small black-and-white photograph of an elderly black woman in a bare room or of an Appalachian family outside a tumbledown shack. Of the modern poor, the mass-market texts usually have something to say that is similar to this passage from Wood, Gabriel, and Biller's *America: Its People and Values:*

> Closely related to the problems of minority groups and civil rights was the problem of poverty in America. Many Americans were affected by poverty, or being poor, but minority groups were especially affected.
>
> In the years following World War II, American prosperity reached an all-time high. Economists said that America was an "affluent society," that is, a nation where people had enough money to live well. But the affluent society was only part of America. There was another part — the America of the poor. According to the government's figures, 12.5 percent of the population was classified as poor in 1971. Americans classified as poor were those lacking enough income to buy the products and services needed for an adequate standard of living.
>
> In the 1970's the American poor were found throughout the nation, in rural areas as well as urban areas. Some of them had no skills and were unable to get jobs. Many were workers who had lost their jobs because new methods of production wiped out many jobs in their industries. . . .
>
> Among the poor were many *migrant farm workers,* that is, workers who migrated, or moved around the country to pick fruit and vegetables. The poor also included farmers who

worked for low wages or for part of the crops they grew, such as farmhands and sharecroppers on Southern farms. These groups also were often made up of minorities — Mexican-Americans, black Americans, Puerto Ricans, and Indians. Perhaps the largest group of the poor were the many older Americans whose only income was their Social Security pension checks.[69]

The passage identifies the poor quite clearly. As a matter of economic analysis, it establishes beyond a shadow of a doubt that the poor are affected by poverty and that poverty is the condition of being without enough income to maintain an adequate standard of living. Other things are less clear. How much is "adequate"? Why does poverty particularly affect people from minority groups? Why do some people work for low wages, and why do some have no skills? There are no answers here, even though the passage raises these questions by its approach. The section goes on to describe, very briefly, President Lyndon Johnson's War on Poverty; it then reports that President Richard Nixon called this war effort a failure, and that he ended some of Johnson's poverty programs and substituted his own revenue-sharing plan. The section concludes:

Ending the federal programs of the 1960's caused some Americans to ask whether problems as difficult as poverty could be solved by government action. Other Americans were convinced that the continued existence of poverty only showed that stronger government programs were needed.[70]

This paragraph, which has its equivalent in all the current best-selling texts, suggests that poverty is a disease, something like cancer. Its cause is unknown, its cure is hotly debated, and yet somewhere — somewhere in the regions yet unprobed by science — there is a vaccine against it. The paragraph suggests that while all Americans dislike poverty, they have only a blunt and perhaps ineffectual instrument called "government" to fight it. This formulation dates back to the texts of the Progressive era, as does the explanation that unemployment is caused by technological advance rather than by any human agency. The text does not, of course, raise the profound question of whether poverty — if only relative poverty — is built into the structure of capitalism. In fact, it does not even suggest that there might be some conflict between the interests of the poor and the interests of the rich. Or that in such conflicts the richest and most powerful groups tend to have disproportionate influence over the government.

The texts are equally evasive or misleading in their social analysis. A number of them have sections in which social scientists discuss such "concepts" as class, status, and social mobility, but these social scientists always manage to avoid the central issues involved in such "concepts," and very often merely succeed in making their own terminology incomprehensible. (One book, for instance, takes as a case study in class structure one of the most egalitarian communities of its day, the Puritans, and reports that the ministers and the magistrates belonged to two different classes. This is rather like saying that Justice Department officials and agents of the F.B.I. belong to two different classes — except that the latter might conceivably be the case.) By playing at economics and sociology in this way, the texts manage to suggest not only that all social scientists are frauds but that intellectual analysis in these matters is useless. With few exceptions, the current texts don't give statistics on income distribution in America or describe the contrasting lives of people in different economic brackets. Many texts suggest that education is the only road to wealth and power — and thus that American society is a mandarinate.

An interesting sidelight on the textbook treatment of the poor is cast by the textbook view of the cities. As short a time ago as the early sixties, the texts carried almost no information about the growth and development of cities in America. At that point, nearly half a century after the urbanization of the country, the texts were describing rural and small-town America as both the condition and the ideal of American life. They mentioned cities merely to describe what was wrong with them — from poor sanitation to political corruption. Only after the urban riots of 1967 did the texts begin to give the cities themselves some attention. This attention is still rather scattered. Current texts discuss the growth of the cities in the late nineteenth century and their condition today. In both periods, the cities seem to be little except a source of problems for the society — air pollution, crime, poverty, and so on. There is no discussion of the importance of cities or the advantages of living in them, nor is there a suggestion that most "city problems," like poverty, are really problems of the nation as a whole.

It is a commonplace to say that the texts of the fifties were superpatriotic — dominated, almost to the exclusion of all else, by the concerns of the Cold War. But it is now hard to remember exactly what this meant, or how it happened. It is interesting, therefore, to watch the ideological drift as it crossed over the subsequent junior-high-school texts of the mid-century. First published in 1931, Casner and Gabriel's *Exploring American History* has had a life span of almost fifty years and was for much of the time a best-selling American history for seventh and eighth graders. Initially, at least, it was the product of a collaboration between a Yale history professor, Ralph Henry Gabriel, and a West Haven, Connecticut, schoolteacher, Mabel B. Casner. According to its first editor, at Harcourt Brace, it did well in the market because of its thematic approach to American history and its "ingenious" teaching strategies.[71]

The first edition is clearly the work of liberals, and it has more than a touch of John Dewey about it. The foreword states that history should be "socially helpful" and should lead to "an understanding of how the life about us has evolved out of the life of the past." The text begins by drawing a parallel between a child's exploration of his own world and the wanderings of an imaginary knight over medieval Europe — the point of which is to explain "why did Europeans wait 500 years to discover America again?" It goes on to draw a picture of pre-Colonial North American Indian life in a manner so stylized that it might have been taken from the backdrop of a case in the American Museum of Natural History. The forest is deep, birds are flitting, squirrels are chattering, and so forth. The Indians, so the book says, were "deeply religious," the proof being that they worshipped so many different spirits; their tragedy was that they had no domestic animals, and therefore "could not progress toward a higher way of life." There are a certain number of poor people in the book — Jacob Riis is mentioned and there is a drawing of the immigrant boats — and very little chauvinism. The War of 1812 is said to have been won by no one, and the Mexican War to have occurred because President James Polk wanted to buy some empty land from the Mexicans and the Mexicans, though poor, were too proud to sell it. Such attempts at balance run through the narrative. The book reports that the United States was "drawn into" world affairs before the First World War, and in the title of the last foreign-policy chapter it asks, "What Steps Has the United States Taken Recently to Promote International Peace?" (a question that provides a perfect logical parallel to "When did you stop beating your wife?").

The 1938 edition of Casner and Gabriel has a new title, *The Rise of American Democracy*, and is said to be a complete reworking of the original volume. It has a new rationale. In their foreword, the authors say that democracy is now being challenged by other forms of government, including "swift-striking dictatorships," and that we therefore have to ask, "What does the word, *democracy*, mean?" The book never quite gets around to answering this question, but its focus is more political than that of the first edition, and its tone more urgent. The story of the knight in the first chapter has been condensed, and the American scenery of birds, squirrels, and leafy boughs has largely disappeared. The Indians are now said to have practiced democracy, not religion; they are no longer "deeply religious." Jacob Riis is still around, but the United States government has become a much more positive actor in social reform. Whereas a mid-thirties edition seems to judge some of President Franklin Roosevelt's legislation to have been unconstitutional, this one simply credits him with having helped the country out of the Depression. In foreign policy, too, the government has taken a positive role: it "helps" the Allies in the First World War and "promotes" world peace thereafter, within the limits of its isolationist position. In the last part of the book, "American Democracy Faces a Confused World," the text maintains that Americans now have new ideals, including a balanced economy, Social Security, and well-being for all citizens. But it ends, rather ominously, "The struggle still goes on. It was never more intense than in our day. The outcome will depend upon the intelligence and alertness of this generation and of future generations."

The 1942 edition, now called *The Story of American Democracy*, has an update on the Second World War and a new preface that refers to the "perilous times" we are living in. Apparently because of this emergency, the Indian sections have been condensed. (They drop out completely in subsequent editions.) In the central part of the book, the titles have changed, and these give a rather different tone to the book. Where once there were "problems" to "challenge democracy," there is now only progress: "American Life Becomes Better for the Common Man," and so on. The Constitutional period is headed "Free Americans Organize a Strong Democratic Nation," and the words "freedom" and "strength" crop up a lot elsewhere. In the last chapter — a completely new one, entitled "The United States Fights for Its Life and for a Free, Democratic World" — there is a photograph caption that reads, "This picture shows citizens enjoying the democratic privilege of free discussion. . . . The leader is helping them to carry on their business in an orderly way." The photograph shows several men on a dais facing a seated audience; it is clearly a meeting of some sort. In contrast to the final worryings of the 1938 edition, this book ends on a note of optimism concerning air travel.

Over the next eight years, the authors — or whoever did the revising of the text — must have felt justified in their optimism, for the 1950 text is a victorious book. The United States now "leads the struggle for democracy"; it has "faced problems," "met challenges"; it has risen "to a position of world leadership" and become "a bastion of the free nations." All of this is, of course, in the twentieth century, but retrospectively the nation has made other gains as well — notably in its nineteenth-century wars. It has not exactly won the War of 1812, but the war is now said to have helped "build the nation." (In earlier editions, the war, less grandly, "develops national feeling.") The Mexican War, which in the first two editions brought the country only empty land, now has brought it vast territories rich in oil and precious metals. In addition, the country has become more prosperous: there are no more poor people or bad social conditions. Pages have been added explaining the superiority of the American democratic system to the Russian police state.

In accordance with the authors' new belief that "perhaps the most important event of the first half of the twentieth century was the rise of the United States to a position of world leadership," the last quarter of the book deals mainly with foreign affairs. These sections portray the United States as playing an essentially benevolent and pacific role in the world. The nation is always attempting to improve communications with the Soviet Union and to "gain peace by mutual understanding" — this in spite of continual rebuffs. In an echo of the liberal internationalism of the first edition, the book talks about the need for international control of atomic energy and the effort to remove the causes of war through the United Nations. The last section, "Democracy Enriches the Lives of Americans," confidently describes recent "advances" in art, education, and science, and points up the American belief in the importance of the individual, of whatever race or creed.

Five years later, this confidence has evaporated; the book is a bundle of anxieties. In the first place, the authors no longer appear to believe that the United States exerts "world leadership." In their foreword, they say that the United States leads "those people in the world who believe in freedom" (a worrying kind of group), and that it is "locked in a struggle" with "another powerful world leader . . . the Soviet Union." Faced with the need to prepare "young people" for the "struggle" in a "complicated and often dangerous world," the authors propose to compare the Russian and American ways of life — American history apparently being of no use anymore. Later on in the book, the authors fulfill their promise by giving an account of Soviet institutions. In this section, one is told that "Russia" is a police state, where "the leader of the Communist party has absolute power over . . . every person." (The book cautiously does not name this leader; Stalin had died two years before publication.) Russia, one learns, is a "fake democracy" and a "fake republic"; worse yet, its industry is geared not to the production of television sets but to war production. In addition, one learns that Russia is tremendously powerful — perhaps even more powerful than the United States, because, in spite of all the American aid to free nations, Russia has managed to block progress and block the growth of prosperity. It is now threatening the free world. (In this section, there is a map of the world color-coded to show which nations are "Communist," which are "free," and which are "neutral." This map classifies all of Indo-China and all of sub-Sahara Africa as "free" and classifies Saudi Arabia, Iran, and most of Latin America, including Mexico, as "neutral." This assessment is mysterious, since the book appeared a year after Dien Bien Phu, several years before the decolonization of most of Africa, and some time after the C.I.A. had brought the Shah of Iran to power and had overturned the Arbenz government in Guatemala.) Internationally, nothing is safe from the Communists, and the home front is not very secure, either. The United States may be a free country, with "wonderful machines" and a free-enterprise system (over which the government now presides in the much reduced capacity of referee), but the Russians are in the process of undermining it. They have already stolen American state secrets through Alger Hiss and the Rosenbergs. They lie a lot, and the Communist Party in the United States espouses violent, undemocratic means. The book therefore approves of the Internal Security Act, the Loyalty Board, and the firm hand of J. Edgar Hoover in the F.B.I.

The most surprising thing about this 1955 edition is the attitude that its authors take toward children. In the thirties editions, they had tried to engage their young readers with adventure stories and romance; here they do nothing but lecture — as if the children might turn out to be small subversives. The last page, subheaded "A Citizen's Rights and Duties," is terribly stern. A citizen's duties, they warn, include military service, jury duty, and paying taxes without cheating. The last few pages — usually given over to science and technology — now include a warning against "false news" and "dangerous propaganda." What the authors are referring to here can only be conjectured, since they are no more explicit than they were when they warned in an earlier section against the questionable practices of "some investigating committees of Congress" — surely the House Un-American Activities Committee and Senator Joseph R. McCarthy's subcommittee. But these two things are probably connected, because the authors offer this explicit piece of advice:

The FBI urges Americans to report directly to its offices any suspicions they may have about Communist activity on the part of their fellow Americans. The FBI is expertly trained to sift out the truth of such reports under the laws of our free nation. When Americans handle their suspicions in this way, rather than by gossip and publicity, they are acting in line with American traditions.[72]

What this paragraph literally says is that an American tradition is that of the police informer. The authors, however, appear to have thought of the F.B.I. as the liberal alternative to the McCarthy subcommittee.

This edition of Casner and Gabriel was not untypical of the texts of the period — certainly in its emphasis on the Communist threat. Virtually all the texts of the mid-fifties made the same estimates of Soviet power and Soviet aggressiveness in foreign policy. Virtually all of them expressed similar doubts about the survival of democracy in this country. The texts of the early forties had not portrayed the Nazis as half so aggressive, or the Second World War as half such a threat to the country. Now the danger was everywhere, invisible. According to Bragdon and McCutchen, one of the most respectable of the high-school texts of the period:

Unquestioning party members are found everywhere. Everywhere they are willing to engage in spying, sabotage, and the promotion of unrest on orders from Moscow.

And

Agents of the worldwide Communist conspiracy have been active inside the United States. Some of them have been trusted officials of the State Department, regularly furnishing information to Russia. Others have passed on atomic secrets; still others have even represented the United States in the UN.[73]

Bragdon and McCutchen were quoting Senator McCarthy and representing his charges as true.

The subversion anxieties of the texts peaked in the mid-fifties, subsiding gradually after that. The early-sixties texts did not repudiate McCarthy except by saying, "Some Americans said there was too much fuss being made about the Communists since there were so relatively few in the United States," or "The struggle divided us when we should have been united." Only now do some texts actually denounce McCarthy's "scare tactics" and take issue with the general assessment of the Soviet Union in the fifties. The aspect of fifties texts that persisted most strongly into the sixties was a certain tone of grimness toward children, and particularly toward young children. It was the junior-high-school books, rather than the high-school ones, that gave such warnings as "Some forces in the world today want to abolish freedom. [But] your heritage as an American provides you with the ideals and faith to give you strength to preserve the rights that are yours as a free American. It is your duty to preserve these rights."[74] And so on. Since these books never defined what they meant by "freedom," the burden they laid on children was truly awesome.

To have been an editor of one of the mass-market texts in the mid-sixties must have been a nightmare — a pit-and-pendulum dilemma — because of the Vietnam War. The problem for editors then was to find a compromise formula that would not offend anyone, when there was no compromise position and no way to avoid the whole subject. The marks of their struggles must give anyone who has read a good number of texts a distinct sense of schadenfreude. In the 1967 edition of Henry F. Graff's *The Free and the Brave*, Graff, or his editors at Rand McNally, came up with the courageous conclusion "One thing was certain: although the United States and its South Vietnamese allies were stuck in a cruel war, the United States showed no signs of abandoning the fourteen million South Vietnamese."[75] This one thing was not so certain less than two years later, when the United States began withdrawing troops from Vietnam, but Rand McNally was stuck with it until 1972, when its editors could cut that sentence and write, "The cease-fire did not hold. But at least the United States was out of the war. And for the first time in a dozen years, no American in uniform was exposed to death in battle anywhere in the world." (What happened to the South Vietnamese the book does not say.)

The 1967 editions, in particular, show signs of editorial difficulties. The Houdini Award for the year must surely go to Nathaniel Platt and Muriel Jean Drummond (or their editors at Prentice-Hall), who concluded their treatment of Vietnam in *Our Nation from Its Creation* by writing:

> Plain people and world leaders fear that such crises as the Vietnam crisis might result in a nuclear war. In an unprecedented appearance before the UN in New York in 1965, Pope Paul VI declared "Never again war! Peace, it is peace which must guide the destinies . . . of all mankind." Again and again President Johnson has indicated that he prays for peace. However, he insists that surrendering South Vietnam to the Vietcong would only lead to more wars.[76]

The masterstroke was to bring in the Pope and to let President Johnson make the final squirm before the holocaust.

One might suppose that writing the history of the war would be rather easier these days, now that the war is over. But in most texts the reporting on the war is no more accurate than their predictions about it were. The majority of the best-selling texts still have no firm grip on Vietnamese geography or nomenclature. Many of them identify the Vietcong as "the military arm of the National Liberation Front" — which is something like calling "the Rebels" the military arm of the Confederacy. Lewis Paul Todd and Merle Curti's *Rise of the American Nation* has found something called "the Communist state of Vietminh" above the seventeenth parallel.[77] Nearly all the texts believe that the Geneva accords of 1954 divided Vietnam into two countries (but then that was what the State Department used to say), and most of them misspell Vietnamese place names. Many mention the Pentagon Papers, but generally contradict what they say. For example, only one narrative text correctly explains that the Johnson Administration provoked the Tonkin Gulf incident by sending South Vietnamese vessels to raid North Vietnamese–held islands. The rest simply state that North Vietnamese boats attacked the *Maddox*; or they say that Johnson "claimed" that an attack on the *Maddox* occurred — leaving the facts of the matter just as mysterious as they were to the United States Senate when it approved the Tonkin Gulf Resolution. The My Lai massacre is another area of dispute. Gerald Leinwand's *Pageant of American History* says that North Vietnamese civilians were killed at My Lai — Leinwand, or his editors at Allyn & Bacon, having in effect moved the village and credited Lieutenant William Calley with a single-handed invasion of North Vietnam.[78] But John Edward Wiltz, in his *The Search for Identity: Modern American History,* doubts whether a massacre occurred at all; according to him, or to his editors at J. B. Lippincott, "the alleged incident at My Lai afforded Communists and anti-Americans everywhere an opportunity to condemn the United States and draw attention away from the countless atrocities which Communists had committed against the civil [*sic*] population of South Vietnam."[79]

Only one narrative text that I can find explains the war in a way that would be plausible to anyone who opposed it. *A People and a Nation,* by Clarence L. Ver Steeg and Richard Hofstadter, calls its Vietnam section unequivocally "The Disaster in Vietnam." In its brief account of the war, it treats the United States government as the principal actor, and says that President Johnson took the decision to commit American troops on the basis of a belief in the domino theory. It states, quite simply, that "large numbers" of Vietnamese opposed the incompetent and repressive government backed by the United States and opposed the "intrusion of Western aliens into their society." It illustrates the tremendous damage that American military forces did to Vietnam (there are pictures of a mangrove forest before and after defoliation) and says that the war polarized American society.[80] In addition, two of the inquiry texts (*As It Happened: A History of the United States,* by Charles G. Sellers et al., and *Discovering American History,* by Allan O. Kownslar and Donald B. Frizzle) include documents that might lead the student to the same kind of conclusion. The first text contains an excerpt from a speech by Senator J. William Fulbright, a report by Jonathan Schell on Operation Cedar Falls, and statements by Johnson and Nixon justifying the American policy; the second conducts a real inquiry into the significance of the Pentagon Papers.[81]

All the rest of the texts are neither hawkish nor dovish on the war — they are simply evasive. Since it is really quite hard to discuss the war and evade all the major issues, their Vietnam sections make remarkable reading. The authors or their editors have had to invent a set of completely original political theories. On the questions why the war began and why it went on for so long, many texts adhere to what might be called the crabgrass theory, the key to which is the avoidance of active combatants as subjects. According to these texts, the war kept on growing until it became "full-fledged"; many Americans were "deeply troubled" by it; and yet, in spite of temporary halts in the bombing of North Vietnam, in spite of appeals to the North Vietnamese leaders, and in spite of negotiations and troop withdrawals, the war kept on going — until it finally stopped.[82] A number of other popular texts use a variant of this theory which puts the blame for the war's duration on the North Vietnamese. Books such as Wiltz and Todd, Curti, for example, chronicle the war as a series of peace overtures by the United States government. Presidents Johnson and Nixon and Secretary of State Henry Kissinger, they say, kept trying to make peace, but the North Vietnamese — for reasons unexplained — refused to stop fighting.[83] Just what anyone's war aims were and why the United States did not simply withdraw its troops from this bellicose little country are questions never confronted. The texts explain the war with the logic of the Red Queen. According to Current, DeConde and Dante, "the United States . . . spent most of a decade working to resolve conflicts in Asia."[84]

For a time during the late sixties, the texts gave a certain amount of space — picture space, mostly — to the antiwar demonstrations in the United States. The peace demonstrators, like the marchers for women's rights and black civil rights, looked clean, kempt, and friendly. These pictures gave no sense of the intensity of the emotions involved or the violence that sometimes accompanied them. The current texts, understandably, contain fewer such pictures. Many, however, contain no reference, or almost none, to the peace movement or to any of the political turmoil of the late sixties and early seventies. In the future, this slate may be wiped clean, as Noam Chomsky is now predicting: the domestic conflicts may disappear along with the issues that gave rise to them, leaving the impression that Americans in the sixties were always united behind their government, and that the war stopped because President Nixon and Secretary Kissinger decided that it should.

For the moment, though, the texts are floundering — and not only with respect to Vietnam. Their evasiveness about the war is just one example of their inability to make sense of American foreign policy, and a mere signal of their deep confusion about the place of the United States in the world. Until the early sixties, the texts had a picture of the world — a single image — that showed the relationship of the United States to other countries. While the details changed (the United States "made peace" or "grew stronger"), the essential outline did not — though reality drifted farther and farther away from it. By the mid-sixties, their single image explained current events only in the way that the Ptolemaic system explained the universe known to Copernicus: there were far more exceptions than rules. After Vietnam, the most literate of the texts abandoned the earlier explanation; the junior-high-school and mass-market texts, however, clung to it, and the result was chaos in the world.

From American-history textbooks over the years, one would gather that foreign policy — or, to put it another way, the rest of the world — became important to the United States only in the nineteen-fifties. The texts published before the fifties gave a maximum of one unit in twelve to American foreign relations. Even those published during or just after the Second World War did not dwell on the subject for long. The texts of the mid-forties dealt with the First World War as an incident and with the Second World War rather briefly and cheerfully, as if it were a distant football game. Thereafter, the emphasis on foreign policy increased steadily, to the point where in the mid-fifties the texts gave from fifteen to twenty per cent of their pages to American relations with the rest of the world. As might be expected, the bulk of the new material concerned foreign relations after 1940, and it was the last quarter or so of every book that sprouted new sections called "The U.S. Broadens Its Horizons" or "The U.S. Assumes World Leadership." These new sections became a standard feature of textbooks and, finally, as much a part of the conventional structure of American history as the chapters on the Revolution and the Constitutional period. Until the mid-seventies, when domestic issues began to crowd these sections off the end pages, foreign policy appeared to be the most important part of modern American history.

The fifties texts, of course, had a rather idiosyncratic view of American relations with the rest of the world. In the context of the Cold War, paranoia reigned. In every other context, this paranoia turned into a militant self-righteousness. According to these books, the United States had been a kind of Salvation Army to the rest of the world: throughout history, it had done little but dispense benefits to poor, ignorant, and diseased countries. In the nineteenth century and the beginning of the twentieth, it had opened doors for the Chinese, saved Cuba from the Spanish, protected Puerto Rico, separated Panama from Colombia in order to wipe out yellow fever, and taken on the Philippines in order to "educate" and "civilize" the Filipinos — just as President William McKinley said. American motives were always altruistic. Even Manifest Destiny "was more than an unconscious movement of people," according to one text. "It also stemmed from pride in American institutions and the desire to spread them as quickly as possible."[85] In the twentieth century, the United States had spent most of its time — apart from a short period of isolation — saving Europe and Asia from militarism, Fascism, and Communism. These efforts had been particularly spectacular after the Second World War. Speaking of that period, Bragdon and McCutchen quoted a nameless group of Oxford scholars as saying, "We are too little astonished at the unprecedented virtuousness of U.S. foreign policy, and at its good sense."[86] (The book came out just after the Korean War and two or more C.I.A.-sponsored coups in the Middle East, and during the period when the government espoused the doctrine of massive retaliation.)

In the fifties texts, there was a tone of innocent wonder about the fact of American power — and a number of strangely naïve attempts to prove its existence. Bragdon and McCutchen again quoted the nameless Oxford scholars to the effect that the United States had been the best "top nation" in history since Rome — thereby acknowledging the superior authority of the British in such matters.[87] The 1957 edition of Muzzey reported:

> The visits of kings, presidents and premiers from many nations give Washington an international significance. Chiefs of state from England, France, India, Japan, Pakistan, Ceylon, Ethiopia, Greece, West Germany, Italy, Austria, Korea, Liberia, Indonesia and Iran joined the steady stream of official guests of our President and Secretary of State. The men and women upon whose leadership depends the destiny of millions of peoples the world over increasingly consulted with the chosen representatives of our way of life.[88]

The paragraph recalls a favorite film of the North Korean embassies of the early seventies, which showed an hour-and-a-half-long procession of foreign dignitaries coming to shake the hand of Kim Il Sung.

How is one to explain this curious mixture of attitudes — this naïve chauvinism, this self-righteousness, and this underlying insecurity? At the time, of course, these emotions were not merely textbook emotions. The texts were reflecting the political temper of the period. But this, too, has to be explained. The American position in the world had changed suddenly and dramatically in the wake of the Second World War. But why this particular reaction? Here the older textbooks are of some help, since they show by comparison which attitudes were new and which belonged to the conventional American wisdom on foreign policy.

The older textbooks reveal, for example, that the chauvinism of the fifties was a new development — at least, chauvinism in that particular degree. The nineteenth century had its chauvinist reactions, but in the eighteen-nineties textbook ardors seemed to cool. From 1900 on, text writers had kept their distance from a good number of American foreign-policy ventures. The Mugwump writers had, for example, portrayed the War of 1812 as an unnecessary muddle created by the shortsightedness of the British and the greed of the American war hawks, with the mess compounded by strategic snafus and resulting in no particular advantage to anyone. The many New England writers of the period disapproved of the Mexican War and frankly characterized American ventures in the Caribbean and the Pacific in the eighteen-nineties as imperialistic. The texts of the thirties were rather more accepting of American expansion to the Pacific but with regard to Europe they tended to reflect a modified Wilsonianism. They described the First World War as a product of imperialism, militarism, and the greed of arms manufacturers, and called for coöperation between nations. As for the texts of the forties, they explained that the Latin-American nations had certain legitimate grievances against the United States. With certain exceptions, the texts of the first five decades of the century did not propose any radical line of dissent from United States foreign policy; still, none went so far as to call every American military venture an unqualified success or suppress information about domestic opposition to the various government initiatives.

Nevertheless, certain elements of the fifties description of the world were completely traditional to textbook history. The idea that the United States was a pure, high-minded nation and a model of virtue among sinners went back to the early nineteenth century, and even further — to the Protestant notion of an elected people. The early textbook writers had justified the American Revolution by citing the peculiar virtues of Americans. Chief among these virtues was innocence of the corruption of money and power. From Emma Willard to David Saville Muzzey, the New England preachers and teachers — whose family fortunes so often came from the triangular trade, as it was known, between Africa, the West Indies, and America, in rum and slaves or the China trade in opium, porcelain, and tea — rarely mentioned American business interests abroad. Whether they favored or opposed American imperial adventures, they invariably did so on the higher ground of the morality or legality of the enterprise. Was the Mexican War moral? Was American dominion over Puerto Rico or the Philippines going to provoke a constitutional crisis? The preachers and teachers from New England had managed by an act of intellectual transcendence to detach themselves from the Yankee traders who established their trust funds. Much as they hated the new Western money, they were no more forthcoming about the American plantations in the Philippines or Hawaii than they were about their own interests. American business abroad was a taboo subject in the Progressive era, just as it was in the nineteen-fifties. It remains taboo today, in spite of the critical approach that some texts take to American military ventures in Asia.

Besides the notion of American altruism abroad, another traditional theme underlay the fifties vision of the world, and that was the theme of American isolation. Of the two, this was the more important, since the other could not have existed without it, and since it was not a statement so much as a picture of the world, from which all statements of foreign policy derived. American-history texts published over the last century have portrayed the English colonies as standing quite alone at the edge of a vast — indeed, continental — wilderness. The earlier texts painted a different picture. Emma Willard and her contemporaries described the frontier as a fairly crowded and war-torn place — a country disputed by the French, the Spanish, the English, various Indian nations, and later the Canadians and the Americans. Then, in the late nineteenth century, the text writers, telescoping the Colonial period into one or two chapters and making it a mere introduction to the history of the United States, stopped writing the history of these conflicts, and so left the impression that "the Americans" went forth into a land without people or previous history — a geographical area as empty and vague as the space beyond a child's vision. True, the texts said that the Spanish conquistadors came to the New World a century before the English settlers, but the same texts dismissed the Spanish settlements in a few paragraphs, and so made it sound as if John Smith had followed on the heels of Pizarro and, once the *Mayflower* arrived, the Spanish had packed up their galleons and gone home. After that, by their account, the wagon trains moved westward into a great emptiness of mountains and deserts, meeting no one except a few wretched Indians. In the late eighteen-forties, the United States fought a border war with the Mexicans, and at the end of the century it went to the aid of the Cubans and the Puerto Ricans.

In part, this vision of the New World was merely a matter of emphasis: the texts were recording the history of a nation-state, not of a people or a continent, and the United States did begin with the English colonies and expand from east to west into a relatively empty continent. Still, a history text prepared by Latin Americans which dealt with the same places and periods would contain too many surprises. In terms of United States history, it is perhaps merely interesting that the oldest European settlement in the New World was on the island of Hispaniola. But it is more than interesting that a map showing Spanish settlements at the time of the American Revolution in what is now the United States would show a fairly heavy sprinkling of cities and towns. (One current textbook includes such a map, and it is the first one to explain why so many cities in California and throughout the Southwest have Spanish names.)

Taken together with the facts about cultural and scientific institutions in Mexico City before the Revolution, this historical geography constitutes an indictment against the textbook writers — of immodesty at best and of concealment at worst. The New World was not quite so new or half so empty as they made out. Far from bringing the first light of European civilization to an unexplored continent, the English colonists came in a rather belated second (or third, since the French got to many places ahead of them). Then in the heroic period of the Founding Fathers the citizens of the new United States were a rough and uncultured lot by comparison with the Spanish. Hispanophobia is partly to blame for this false impression of American singularity and isolation on an empty continent. But so, perhaps, is the mental geography of the Easterners who wrote so many of the textbooks and created their conventions. Writers such as Muzzey and Albert Bushnell Hart had no real feeling for the West even after "the Americans" got there. These men's sense of space ran backward, as it were, across the Atlantic. Europe was the only geographical reality, and the European nations were the only peers of the United States. But here there was a gap, a lack of connection, for Europe was by definition the place that Americans had left behind. The same writers who insisted on

Americans' roots in Europe wrote as if the United States had no further relationship with the European powers after the Revolution. They wrote as if throughout the nineteenth century the United States had no foreign relations to speak of.

The mid-twentieth-century habit of skipping from the War of 1812 to the Mexican War to the Spanish-American War, with a brief jab at the Louisiana Purchase and the Monroe Doctrine, is not a new ellipsis, resulting from new pressures on space. It is the traditional textbook way of reporting American foreign relations in the nineteenth century. Of course, there is some truth to the current conventional wisdom that nations have become increasingly interdependent — and to its implication that they had more autonomy in the past. At the same time, it is hard to think of anything more fundamental to the United States in the nineteenth century than its relationship with Europe. To begin with, General Washington could hardly have sustained the Revolutionary War during its early years if it had not been for the gunrunning operation financed by the French and Spanish governments. The fact is merely exemplary, for until the First World War the United States was a debtor nation. In the arts, in science, and in most forms of intellectual life, the United States was a mere province of Europe.

Of course, to define the American relationship with Europe is to see why the nineteenth- and early twentieth-century writers rarely discussed it. Indebtedness is never very encouraging to contemplate, and the task of American historians, as they saw it, was giving their new country an independent existence. Yet this denial of Europe went on long after it had become quite clear that the United States had done very well out of the relationship. At the time of the First World War, even the committed Anglophiles, such as Muzzey and Hart, never explained American economic or strategic interests in Europe. The text writers of the thirties and forties did little better, for, with all their talk about militarism, Fascism, and so forth, they did not acknowledge United States interests in or influence upon the European economy and balance of power. Even the seventies texts do not say that the Great Depression originated in the United States and spread throughout the world, nor do they show a link between the Depression and the rise of Fascism in Europe. Only one book I have found — Wiltz's *The Search for Identity: Modern American History* — reports that immigrants came from Scandinavia in the eighteen-eighties and from southern Italy in the eighteen-nineties in part because the United States had, by increasing its agricultural production, taken away their markets and their livelihoods.[89]

From the eighteen-nineties to the nineteen-fifties, the texts had portrayed the United States as isolated not only by the small quantity but by the meagre quality of its relationships with other countries, for what was reported was only wars and territorial acquisitions. To many generations of American children, it must therefore have appeared that Americans were just as those cosmopolitans Jefferson and Franklin had painted them: naïve, untutored in the wiles of foreign trade — rugged individualists, economically speaking. It must also have seemed to such children that the United States had always acted unilaterally — had never engaged in diplomacy, and had never had a beneficial, or even a cordial, relationship with any other country. The maintenance of this fiction through two world wars and a worldwide depression explains a good deal about the attitudes of the fifties texts — this strange combination of a naïve sense of power and virtue with a sense of powerlessness against invisible enemies. The United States was the young Siegfried, magically strong, and innocent of the burdens of history, yet at the same time an orphan, surrounded by potential enemies in an unrecognizable world. The change from the thirties vision of the United States as the peacemaker in European quarrels over money and arms to the fifties vision of the United States as the sole champion of freedom in the world is not in fact very great.

By the mid-sixties, the texts no longer deduced foreign affairs from the principle that the Soviet Union controlled a worldwide conspiracy. With the abatement of their anxiety about subversion came an end to the flat statements about the virtue of America and to the long discussions of the nature of the Soviet state. (Presumably, even children now knew that the Communists were the bad guys — if not exactly why.) Just as the Soviet Union was completing its economic recovery from the Second World War and developing a nuclear capability to match that of the United States, the texts seemed to lose much of their interest in it. By the early sixties, their focus had shifted from Europe to Asia, and to a new series of threats. The major threat seemed to be the Chinese Communists, or the "Red Chinese" — to whom "we" had unaccountably "lost China."* They had fought United Nations troops in Korea and were now "turning their attentions" to Vietnam. And there were other, unidentified Communists threatening the freedom of other countries — Indonesia, Laos — which had never before been mentioned in American-history texts but were now said to be of vital importance. The enemy,

* For example, Graff and Krout, *The Adventure of the American People* (1959), page 650, says, "The loss of China was particularly galling to many here. . . ."

it appeared, was horribly elusive. But, said the texts, the United States was meeting these challenges by forming alliances. (The mid-sixties texts were tremendously respectful of all John Foster Dulles's pacts, from SEATO to CENTO, and many of them went to the trouble of drawing these creations onto world maps.) While the Russians "curried favor" with the underdeveloped countries, the United States gave "billions of dollars in aid" to help these countries and make them strong. Forging alliances was not an easy task, however, for these countries were strangely ungrateful. The liberal Graff and Krout text said gloomily that America "must learn to acquire the friendship" of these countries, an undertaking that it said would be expensive and would "not often show tangible or quick returns."

> Americans will have to be aware that there is abroad much anti-American feeling. The feeling grows out of resentment and envy of our place as a Great Power. It also comes from the idea that we have sometimes disregarded the feelings of other people . . .
>
> But we must take our role hopefully and responsibly.[90]

If "world leadership" was not an easy task in the mid-sixties, it became even more uncomfortable as time went on. In revising texts for 1968 and 1969, the editors replaced maps of alliances with maps of "trouble spots," and replaced the half-sanguine descriptions of aid programs with accounts of crises. In the liberal books of the period, American foreign relations seemed to consist solely of crises: in Berlin, China, Korea, Suez, Hungary, Indo-China, the Congo — you name it. Only the Peace Corps remained to give a tiny fifties upbeat to the end of the list. (The Peace Corps, in fact, got an extraordinary amount of mileage. For at least ten years, the texts made it by far the best-known agency of United States foreign policy.) Whereas in the fifties the United States had had one large enemy, it now had innumerable little irritants. Indeed, from the perspective of the textbooks the world was nothing but a mass of countries making trouble for the United States. Why these foreigners were so bothersome and why the United States was "interested in" such far-flung "problem areas" remained mysterious, however. There were crises, that was all, and the United States went about "acting to solve" them. In the course of one decade, the United States had changed from the young Siegfried into Gulliver — or perhaps the White Rabbit, since it was constantly rushing around worrying about crises. The transformation must have surprised any of those brought up on the fifties books who were aware of it, but it left most of the old premises intact: the United States always acted in a disinterested fashion, always from the highest of motives; it gave, never took; though beset by problems, it was still without peer and in all important respects was still alone in the world.

Against this background, a few of the seventies texts are shockingly different in their approach. They ask questions — real questions — about the conduct of foreign policy. The inquiry texts raise these questions directly. *As It Happened*, by Charles Sellers, for instance, contrasts a speech by Senator Barry Goldwater and a speech by Senator Fulbright and then asks, "Was United States foreign policy in the cold-war period that of a 'responsible' champion of freedom or that of an 'arrogant' great power?" The question is a bit too anthropomorphic, even with the quotation marks, to make for good history, but still it raises the very issue that is most firmly settled by the great majority of texts (including, no doubt, the ones that students of this text would have read in junior high school). In an earlier chapter, these authors put together an excellent collage of documents on President Woodrow Wilson's policies during and after the First World War and ask questions designed to make students look at how decisions are made and draw their own conclusions about the relationship between Wilson's goals, his tactics, and the realities of Europe in 1918. Other texts, such as Edwin Fenton's *A New History of the United States: An Inquiry Approach*, discover unpleasantnesses that have rarely been recorded by history texts and are not in general well known — for one, the use of torture by American soldiers in the campaign to pacify the Philippines after the Spanish-American War. All these books at least imply that there are some limits to American power and American virtue.

For a number of the mid-seventies books, the Cold War is now over: it is history, and a rather peculiar part of history at that. The 1974 edition of Kownslar and Frizzle's *Discovering American History* has a startling paragraph on the Truman Doctrine, which begins:

> A serious situation developed in Greece in the years 1946–7. Great Britain tried to reassert its influence in Greece by imposing a reactionary monarchy on the country. This action provoked a bitter civil war in Greece. . . . President Truman . . . felt that if the Communist nationalists won Greece, Turkey would be at the mercy of the Soviet Union. Thus, the balance of power in the Middle East as well as in Europe would be drastically changed.

The book quotes a passage from the Truman speech to Congress that became known as the Truman Doctrine, and then concludes:

> This Presidential statement committed the United States to intervene in revolutions anywhere in the world. Some historians believe that Truman's policy was not wise. They feel that it drew the United States into situations over which American leaders had little or no real control, and that Truman made no distinction between real military threats to American interests and revolutions which arose from local conditions.[91]

The passage is particularly striking in view of the fact that the 1967 edition of the same book says of the same event simply:

> To combat Communism, Congress appropriates $400 million for military and economic aid to Greece and Turkey. President Truman says, "I believe that it must be the policy of the United States to support free peoples who are resisting attempted subjugation by armed minorities or by outside pressures."[92]

These new, critical texts are far from left-wing in their orientation. Many of their criticisms — like the one of the Truman Doctrine — represent a distinctly conservative point of view. None of them have so much as broached the subject of American economic interests abroad. And, obviously, almost none of them have yet mentioned such "controversial" subjects as the multinational corporations, the military-industrial complex, or the C.I.A. Except in the most sophisticated of the books — like Sellers' *As It Happened* — there is never any attention given to the perspective of other governments. What is radical about the books is that they question the judgments of past Presidents and Administrations, and, in the process, make it clear that foreign policy is not some mysterious emanation of the national will but the actions of certain people operating within a certain historical context. For the first time since the end of the First World War, foreign policy appears in textbook history as something less than a sacred revelation.

This critical view is far from universal, and many of the texts remain true to an early-sixties vision of the world. One of the most popular of the texts — Howard B. Wilder, Robert P. Ludlum, and Harriett McCune Brown's *This Is America's Story* — still does not acknowledge the Sino-Soviet split, even though it now approves of President Nixon's trip to China.[93] Another one — Todd, Curti — still portrays the world as a mass of trouble spots and crisis areas with foreigners making trouble for us.[94] These spots are now so numerous that American foreign policy looks completely chaotic and senseless. The old image of American isolation remains, but, as with the Ptolemaic picture of the universe in Copernicus's day, the exceptions overwhelm the rules.

For some reason, the books for junior-high-school children tend to be more chauvinistic and more macho than the high-school books. Wood, Gabriel, and Biller, for instance, says, "Victory in the Spanish-American war called world attention to the growing power of the United States. America had won a great victory. In the future, the United States would be treated as the great nation it had become."[95] In fact, the less literate the designated audience, the more pugnacious the books. In Jerome R. Reich and Edward L. Biller's *Building the American Nation* — a junior-high-school text clearly intended for black inner-city children — America is always "growing stronger" or "gaining respect," and its foreign policy seems to be exclusively a matter of "fighting dictatorships," "fighting Communism," and so on. Granted that the reading level of these books precludes a sophisticated analysis of foreign policy, there is still no obvious reason for such attitudes. The chauvinism of these books is particularly mysterious in view of the fact that the elementary-school social-studies books have, if anything, gone overboard in the other direction. Harcourt Brace Jovanovich, the publisher of the two history texts just mentioned, has a social-studies series for the elementary grades which devotes endless pages to showing that people of the most exotic nationalities, races, creeds, and cultures are all very nice and just as human as American boys and girls. The messages that children must receive are thus rather confusing: love everyone in the elementary grades, fight Communism in junior high, and face endless intractable problems in high school. To put it another way, the answer to the sixties seems to be: educate children of different age groups and of different social classes differently.

To look at all the texts of the seventies together is to wonder whether it is really possible to teach twentieth-century American foreign affairs in the context of American history. The traditional textbook method — exemplified in the junior-high-school texts — is to report the actions of the United States government, the rationale for them, and the consequences. The perspective on any century is absurdly narrow: the American, British, and Canadian textbook accounts of the War of 1812 look like the reports of three of those blind men who tried to describe an elephant. And as a view of the twentieth century it is surreal, since it supposes an eighteenth-century world order in which only governments are actors and in which the executive has full charge of foreign policy. Some of the seventies texts have widened this perspective a good deal: a few present the positions of other governments in terms that those governments would accept, and at least suggest the existence of domestic political or institutional conflict over foreign-policy issues. With this approach, the texts could discuss the Arab-Israeli wars, the Panama Canal Treaties, or the SALT talks without making the Secretary of State ("acting quickly to meet the challenges") look like a participant in the Queen of Hearts' croquet game, and they could discuss the manipulation of other governments by the C.I.A. or by the multinational corporations — only they choose not to. On the other hand, it is difficult to conceive how they could deal with issues like nuclear proliferation, worldwide inflation, and world food shortages without breaking their own frameworks. And yet these matters that are neither quite foreign nor quite policies are just as important to the United States as any matters that are both. The texts do not now, and they cannot, describe the overlap between domestic and foreign affairs or the dense network that connects American society with the rest of the world. (One geography text does this rather well, by looking at all the ways in which Cleveland is linked to other countries. But that relationship is its sole subject.) What this means is that not only traditional textbook approaches but national histories per se have become in many ways outdated. To describe international relations as the sum of a government's foreign policies is to give a false picture of the world. There's nothing to be done about it — national histories have their own intrinsic value — but the fact remains that an American child who will grow up to work for General Motors, the City of New York, or a large wheat farm, say, will find United States history just about as useful as the history of Saxony would have been to a Saxon soldier going off to fight in the Napoleonic Wars.

Progressives, Fundamentalists, and Mandarins

A CASUAL reader of American-history textbooks for elementary and secondary schools might be tempted to conclude that the signal quality of all of them is an astonishing dullness. But this would be unfair, because some texts are not dull at all. The mid-nineteenth-century Peter Parley texts, with their tales of earthquakes and heroic children captured by Indians are, for instance, quite readable compared with the histories of the eighteen-nineties — though, of course, somewhat less factual. The first few editions of David Saville Muzzey's *American History* are full of life, and the anti-Communist tracts of the fifties have a certain hysterical suspensefulness. American-history texts are not, in other words, by their nature dull. They have achieved dullness. And, it must be said, they have maintained a fairly consistent level of dullness ever since the nineteen-thirties. The proposition is inadequate as well as unfair, because the dullness the texts have achieved is neither simple nor self-explanatory. Leonard C. Wood, Ralph H. Gabriel, and Edward L. Biller's description of poverty in *America: Its People and Values* and Lewis Paul Todd and Merle Curti's theory of the Vietnam War in *The Rise of the American Nation* could not have come from mindless drudging or ad-hoc worrying about offense to some group. No, these textbook theories are the product of a coherent world view, a philosophy of history. And this world view emerges if one examines the peculiar quality of the texts' dullness.

To read an account of, say, the American Revolution in one of the so-called inquiry, or discovery, textbooks — which focus on a few topics, illustrate them with documents from primary and secondary sources, and include a list of questions designed to force students to think much as historians do — is to see that the narrative texts, past and present, are dull in part because of their silences. The longest of these silences — it begins with the foundation of the Republic and remains perfect even today — is on the subject of intellectual history. It is not that modern texts are hostile to intellectuals. It is not that at all. Ever since the thirties, text writers have taken to stopping every hundred pages or so to build a section around American cultural achievements. Since the fifties, they have given American writers and artists at least as much space as they give to sports stars, and their works as much space as technological advances in the media. They are not quite as up to date about writers as they are about painters and painting (current texts include Op and Pop Art, but stop with Faulkner and Hemingway), but their literary appreciations are quite sophisticated. (Not since the thirties has a text summed up *Moby Dick* as "a story about a whale.") American art — if not intellectual life in general — has become an attraction, a matter for national pride. Of course, these culture sections do bear some resemblance to what in news magazines is called "the back of the book," and American intellectuals might with some justice complain that they have been ghettoized in them — fenced off by black lines from the serious people and serious concerns of the age. But the problem is really the contrary of that: these serious people who wield political power or influence are never credited by the textbooks with having thought anything. It is, for instance, a well-kept secret of the texts that the

Founding Fathers were intellectuals. But this is the least of it. What is missing is not a history of intellectuals but intellectual history in the broadest sense.

Were a foreigner to read American-history texts (and particularly a foreigner brought up, as the French are, to put Descartes before anyone else), he or she would have to conclude that American political life was completely mindless. For instance, the texts report that Thomas Paine's *Common Sense* was an influential pamphlet without ever discussing what it says. (The fact that Paine was an internationalist who believed that the Revolution would spread back to Europe is another well-kept secret.) Similarly, they report that the Populists represented rural interests, called for government ownership of railroads, and sounded more extreme than they actually were. Of the Populists' highly colored and wholly original view of the world they say nothing. (It is possible to imagine that the radicals of the sixties, such as Tom Hayden and Sam Brown, associated themselves with the Populist tradition because their American histories told them a lot about Robert La Follette and nothing about the rural, reactionary, Catholic-hating, Jew-baiting strain in the movement.) But it is not only radical or currently unfashionable ideas that the texts leave out — it is all ideas, including those of their heroes. In all the texts since Muzzey's, Henry Clay, John Calhoun, and Daniel Webster are stick figures deprived of speech. Even Thomas Jefferson and Alexander Hamilton are insubstantial, their ideas on government reduced to little more than a difference on the merits of a national bank. As for the Puritans, the texts manage to describe that most ideological of communities without ever saying what they believed in.

The lack of intellectual history in the texts has had some

serious consequences, one of which is that students get a rather profound misunderstanding of the Constitution. In discussing that document, the textbooks have traditionally focussed on how it operates and what it has done. Their account of the Constitutional Convention is similarly functional — to the point where the final document appears merely a product of interest-group compromises, a masterpiece of political tinkering. Rarely have they mentioned the political philosophy of the Framers — since the thirties, in any case. Some fifties writers thus made no great break with tradition when they moved the Constitution with all of its modern amendments into the chapter on the Constitutional Convention and there discussed "the American system of government" as if it were a constant preserved in the National Bureau of Standards. Current writers place the text at the back of the book and discuss the constitutional amendments in their proper historical contexts, indicating that the American system has changed to some degree. But since they still do not ground the original document in the political philosophy of the period, they run the opposite risk of making the document appear no more than a collection of rules and regulations — a kind of Rube Goldberg machine, any part of which could be altered to fit circumstances without changing the sense of the whole. In addition to missing the spirit of the law, the texts have surely missed the spirit of American politics by their neglect of intellectual history. The United States has not been — is not yet — a land of philosophers, but it is essentially one of visionaries. People such as Cotton Mather, W. E. B. Du Bois, Henry Ford, and Emma Goldman have given the country its real life force. To deny their visions is to drain the soul out of American history.

The textbook substitute for intellectual history has always been editorial moralizing. In the blood-soaked, battle-ridden texts of the nineteenth century, the authors wrote forewords proclaiming their moral purposes and the virtues the study of American history would instill in young readers. Around the turn of the century, they began moralizing in earnest, passing judgment on everything from the Salem witchcraft trials to the Payne-Aldrich Tariff Act. In place of the real dilemmas of Thomas Jefferson or Abraham Lincoln, they gave students their own views on the good and bad guys and what should have been done. Why they felt so morally competent was not at all clear, but they gave students to understand that history was a series of instructive morality plays. This Victorian view of history — and of children — persisted long after the texts had abandoned people for social forces. It persists today, in spite of the bland neutrality of textbook language.

In the first part of this century, character was the main focus — and source of interest — of the textbooks. American history had heroes and villains, people and even "races" of good and bad character. The best of the writers clearly took pleasure in describing the complexities of personality — particularly if there was a tragic flaw to be found. Muzzey's characterization of Warren G. Harding, for example, might be a piece of movie scriptwriting:

> President Harding was a man of superb figure and physique. He looked "every inch a King." To a Washingtonian dignity in appearance, he added a most un-Washingtonian geniality of manner, a hail-fellow-well-met companionship of the "good mixer" among "the boys" with whom he enjoyed a Saturday night's game of poker. . . . But behind the façade of his handsome face, his genial manners, and his winning voice President Harding had but meagre qualifications for the responsibilities of

the high office to which he had been elected. Both mentally and morally he failed to measure up to high standards . . . his pliant good nature and his attachment to personal friends like the crooked politicians of the "Ohio gang" and plunderers of the public wealth brought discredit upon his administration and bitter sorrow (perhaps even death) to himself.[96]

Since the nineteen-thirties, however, the characters of American history have grown small and pale in the shadow of institutions and social forces. In the 1972 edition of Todd, Curti, President Harding was merely

a genial Ohio newspaperman who had climbed to the top of the political ladder in his own state. Before becoming President he had served as United States Senator in Washington. Handsome and distinguished, with a warm, easygoing manner — much too easygoing, as it turned out — he had many friends in every walk of life. . . .

Despite some solid accomplishments, the Harding administration left a long, sorry record of corruption. President Harding was not himself involved in the corruption. His mistake was in appointing certain undeserving men to office.[97]

Of course, it is no longer possible to write history as if it were merely the play of personalities. And John Dewey, among others, is surely right that to devote much attention to the Presidents or other individual leaders is undemocratic. On the other hand, this neglect of character in the schoolbooks is an aesthetic impoverishment. In the days of Muzzey, American history had gentlemen, shysters, hotheads, statesmen, and fools; it now has only cipher people, who say very little and think nothing — who have no passions and no logic.

It is difficult to write an interesting history for children about impersonal institutions and faceless social forces, but it can be done. Charles and Mary Beard, among others, have demonstrated that it can. What is impossible is to write an interesting history without conflicts of any kind. Yet ever since the thirties the texts have been written without conflicts. Class conflict has always been inadmissible to them — it is un-American. (Willis Mason West's *American History and Government* is the exception that proves the rule.) Racial and religious conflicts went out as soon as the texts discovered there were two sides to them. Current texts, more sensitive than their predecessors on race questions, take the part of minorities by using what might be called the Tinker Bell mode: "Today the first Americans, like many other groups, are organizing to demand full rights. Their activities have led many other Americans to think deeply about the wrongs which the American Indians have suffered." Considering the struggles that the American Indians have recently had with the F.B.I., the mining companies, and the citizens of a number of states — struggles that were reported on television and in the newspapers — this is surely an excess of non-information.

For some time now, the tendency has been to minimize violent confrontations of all sorts. The space given to battles has been diminishing ever since the eighteen-forties — its high point being in the texts of Emma Willard and her contemporaries. Since the nineteen-thirties, the coverage of wars in general has shortened as well — and not just from a military standpoint. The Korean War, with all the important political and constitutional issues it raised, now takes up no more than three or four paragraphs in most books. Several books currently on the market have no wars in them at all. These "warless histories" describe the causes and effects of the major wars but omit all mention of military conflict. In some sense, they are the ultimate reduction to absurdity. On the other hand, they are a good deal more informative than those that report the battles but fail to report the differences that led to them.

In this century, the texts have given vast amounts of space — two chapters, usually — to explaining the causes of the Civil War. They have made that conflict the most important one in American history. Yet a child could not possibly infer from any text written since the thirties the passions that animated the war. Both Confederates and Unionists appear in the texts as perfectly reasonable people without strong prejudices. The conflict between the two economic and social systems is described in language so pallid that it does not begin to convey the meaning of the war for those who were involved. Thus, in spite of the long explanations of the Dred Scott Case and the Missouri Compromise, the causes of the war seem insufficient.

Of course, it is quite likely that in the case of racial and religious groups the text writers avoid mention of conflict in the interest of current social harmony. But in other cases — such as that of the Civil War — where the conflict involves long-dead sectional, economic, or political differences, the avoidance seems to come more from confusion than from deliberation. Having abandoned the notion that individuals make history, the texts seem uncertain as to what really does make history. They have found a great variety of temporary actors — "the North," "the Free World," "the farmers" — but no recurrent ones and no systematic relationships. In most texts, economics seems to have had something to do with the Civil War but nothing to do with, say, the Mexican War or the Second World War. Reading Todd, Curti, one gets the impression that the Fascist dictatorships popped up in the thirties as mysteriously as toadstools after a rain. According to most texts, the Progressive Party just appeared, in the same way, while the Populist Party was founded on the economic grievances of farmers. In discussing recent domestic conflicts, the texts cannot seem to locate any actor except for a vague American public opinion. "Many Americans felt the problem of poverty could not be solved by government action . . . while others felt . . ." exactly the opposite. History is thus not a matter of fact but a matter of the opinions of unnamed, uncounted, and perhaps uninformed citizens.

As a substitute for conflicts between one identifiable thing and another, the texts offer "problems." For example, Todd, Curti has this to say about Reconstruction:

> The era of reconstruction left many major problems unsolved and created a number of new and equally urgent problems. This was true even though many forces in the North and the South were working for the reconciliation of the two sections of the Union.[98]

These "problems" seem to crop up everywhere. History in these texts is a mass of problems — some of them of the most unusual sorts. In life, it is customary for problems to occur before solutions are found, but in the texts this is not always the case. In most current books, the "problem" of poverty appears only in the context of President Lyndon Johnson's war on it, and race discrimination occurs under the heading of the civil-rights movement. Quite often, the texts will find solutions for problems they have not mentioned — for instance, such "solutions" as the Pure Food and Drug Act, the child-labor laws, and the Good Neighbor Policy. The texts do not, of course, reveal which solutions did not succeed, but occasionally they mention new solutions, such as the Alliance for Progress, to old nonproblems. The texts also recognize the existence of certain unsolved problems. Quite a few of these seem to be of a technical nature, such as air pollution and unemployment: ". . . the 1950s brought *automation*, in which machines were developed to operate other machinery. Automation wiped out the jobs of large numbers of unskilled workers."[99] Other problems, like poverty and discrimination, are more mysterious. In any case, no one can be held responsible for problems, since everyone is interested in solving them. In all history, there is no known case of anyone's creating a problem for anyone else. (Not Southerners or Northerners but "the era of Reconstruction" created problems for the post-Reconstruction period.) These "problem areas" resemble a landscape after a neutron bomb has hit, for there are no human agencies left—only abstractions and passive verbs. While the law recognizes victimless crimes, the texts have established the concept of authorless crimes—this to go along with their sideless conflicts.

In all of this, it is possible to discern a philosophy, quite original to the texts, which, in honor of its prototype in the Peter Parley tales of earthquakes, one might call the natural-disaster theory of history. This theory is remarkably comprehensive—it explains almost everything from pollution to the Vietnam War. And it is *the* textbook explanation of Watergate:

> Following his sweeping election victory, President Nixon's second term began with great promise. But soon serious political problems arose. Some of the men who had managed his

reelection campaign had used unlawful methods. They hired burglars to break into the headquarters of the Democratic Party at the Watergate building in Washington, D.C.[100]

This follows Wood, Gabriel, and Biller's account of how Nixon in his first term faced problems in Indo-China and elsewhere. The book goes on to explain that the Watergate scandal severely damaged Nixon's prestige and adds, "The Nixon administration was further weakened when Vice-President Agnew resigned in 1973 after a jury indicted him on charges of income tax evasion." Somehow this text neglects to quote John Dean's statement about the "cancer growing on the Presidency" — for that would have made everything perfectly clear.

The texts in fact arrived at this Natural Disaster theory out of an internal necessity that came with the advent of democratic histories. Muzzey and his contemporaries had conflicts galore in their books, for they had villains as well as heroes, and they could condemn individuals for dastardly acts without condemning the system as a whole. The later texts had, however, only institutions and abstractions to offer. These institutions made rather poor heroes since they were so little expressive ("democracy" could not act the part of, say, Teddy Roosevelt), but they made even worse villains. In fact, with the exception of slavery there were no American institutions or large groups of citizens they could even cast in that role. And without villains there could, in the moralistic world of textbooks, be no conflicts, but only "problems" created by no one.

The moral burden had, of course, to lie somewhere, and in the thirties the texts developed the habit of displacing it from the real offenders onto the heads of children. Their titles for many years implied that students bore the responsibility for the whole of American history. This period of books called "Your Heritage" or "Our Nation from Its Creation" now seems to be over, but the end pages of many current texts still exhort children to "face challenges" and "meet responsibilities." Current texts are slightly more modest than their predecessors in describing the achievements of adults: "We recognize that our government is not perfect; our way of life falls short of what it ought to be." But their demands on children are no less exigent, "these conditions can be improved if each individual does his fair share." History can be of very little help to the student here since — according to all texts published since the turn of the century — this particular moment in history is the most dangerous, critical, or important period in the history of the United States. According to one text published just after Watergate: "Modern science and technology have made the American people the best educated and informed in history. As a result, for the first time in man's history, the fullest achievement of America's values and ideals is possible."

From "The Land of Progress" to "The Rise of the American Nation," the titles of most modern textbooks propose a forward motion to history. In their prefaces text authors are always talking about "charting progress" or, less optimistically, teaching children to "adapt to change." This insistence on motion is ironic, for of all forms of history, the texts describe historical movement less well than any other. Of course any history that performs the service of "covering" the major events of American history in chronological order cannot help but be somewhat static. Still, there is no structural reason why they have to be quite as mosaic as they are. Even those advertised as "thematic" histories do not make the obvious connections between events. Politics is one thing to them, economics another, culture a third. As there is no link between the end of Reconstruction in the South and the civil-rights movement of the sixties, so there is none between Watergate and Vietnam. Because the texts cannot identify the actors in history, they cannot make these connections. Events — wars, political disputes, judicial decisions — simply appear like Athena out of the head of Zeus. And history is just one damn thing after another. It is in fact not history at all.

The discontinuities in textbook history break up the past, but the incessant moralism of the texts dissolves all sense of it for the student. The most progress-oriented of the texts often carry in their front or back pages a list of "American values." One contemporary list goes as follows:

1. Americans value laws and legal principles which change to meet the needs of changing times.
2. Americans value the principle that the nation's armed forces must, at all times, be controlled by civilians.
3. Americans value voluntary public service by individuals to help our citizens at home and to help other peoples abroad.
4. Americans value the use of knowledge to improve people's lives.
5. Americans greatly value the sharing of knowledge.
6. Americans value a democratic sharing of the power of government.
7. Americans value the respect due to each person in our democracy.
8. Excellence is an essential value to Americans.

To the extent that they are not just wishful thinking (and strangely arbitrary wishful thinking at that) these lists are anachronisms — their very existence implies that

American values have not changed at all in the course of four centuries. Some of the new texts do not have lists but instead questions such as "What do you think about President Johnson's plan for Reconstruction? What would you have done in his shoes?" These questions derive from a post-sixties admission that Americans do not think alike on every issue and that therefore the goal of a teacher can be merely to clarify students' ideas, beliefs, and prejudices. These questions are also, however, completely ahistorical.*

The ideology that lies behind these texts is rather difficult to define, because it does not fit the usual political patterns. It is not classical conservatism, since the texts, far from glorifying the past, offer it up as a mere appendage to the present. It is not progressive history, either, for, with all their exhortations to students, the texts never indicate any line of action. Because they do not show historical development in American values and institutions, they deny all possibility of reflection on change in the future. Neither Whig nor Tory, their approach to history is, in fact, more primitive than either philosophy would allow. Their history is a catechism, except that it deals with institutions, not individuals. In its flatness and its uncritical conformism, it is a kind of American Socialist realism.

Happily, there are now other books on the market that have a vastly different approach. Not all of these are inquiry texts; some narrative texts for older children have

* The most glaring example is in *The Americans: A History of the United States*, by the Social Studies Curriculum Center Staff, Carnegie-Mellon University, Edwin Fenton general editor (1975). The book gives a unit to Gabriel Prosser's plan for invading Richmond and freeing the slaves. It says, "As you read Prosser's plan of attack, think about whether or not a man should risk his life to help his fellow men" (page 181). Then on page 183, it says, "People in all our communities today have serious problems, just as slaves had problems before the Civil War. Many of you, your parents and other interested people are working to help those who have problems."

broken the form and show a more or less historical approach to history. But the inquiry books came first; they influenced all the others, and even now they remain the most radically different in educational philosophy. One excellent example of the form is a chapter on the American Revolution in *As It Happened: A History of the United States*, by Charles Sellers et al. That chapter is not a complete history of the Revolution but an examination of the American decision to secede from England. Composed mainly of contemporary documents, it includes portions of the letters or autobiographies of such people as John Adams; Samuel Adams; a Tory delegate to the First Continental Congress; and a Boston loyalist, the sister of the customs commissioner, who witnessed some of the violence surrounding the Boston Tea Party. The authors interpolate these documents with explanatory notes, narrative connections, and a great variety of questions to the student. The questions are those a historian would ask of the material: What is the point of view of the speaker? What can be inferred from his statement? Can you reconcile these conflicting views at any point? What does this say about the ultimate questions of national identity? The questions force the student to take an active role — to examine the evidence, draw conclusions about matters of fact, and develop hypotheses about political behavior. The chapter focusses on conflict and therefore on change. The documentary material gives the student some brush with historical reality — with the characters involved and with the atmosphere of the time. The authors take certain definite positions in their narrative sequences, but they are not at all moralistic. The purpose of the documents and the questions is clearly to show the logic of various positions and to leave the student to analyze and interpret what occurred. History, this chapter demonstrates, is not a catechism to be learned by heart but a mass of conflicting data that must be ordered and interpreted. As for the past, it is much like the present, except that "we" — though we may have our views or passionate opinions — no longer have any direct responsibility for it. The title of Sellers' book, *As It Happened*, expresses this notion perfectly.

Much is implied by the very form of the inquiry texts. While the old-style narratives displayed an essentially medieval state of mind, these new case-study books, with their multiple perspectives, suggest a modernist aesthetic and theory of knowledge. Seventy-odd years after the intellectual revolution led by such men as Einstein, Joyce, and Picasso, at least some educators have seen fit to teach children about it. That said, the inquiry books vary widely in content and in quality. They vary because there is still no pat formula for making them — each one is an original piece of history. Some make an attempt to cover all the usual College-Board-exam issues; others concentrate on selected events in order to show exemplary modes of analysis. Some have fascinating, unconventional selections of documents and well-written narrative connections; others are banal or simply sloppy — they use articles from *Time* or *Newsweek* as commentaries on events, or they include "fictional re-enactments" of historical dramas. The sad thing is that many of them, and parts of nearly every one, do not satisfy the minimum requirements of the methodology and would not pass muster with any respectable historian.

Some of the failings of the inquiry texts are of the sort one might find in the older narrative texts. Virtually all the inquiry texts include questions that are irrelevant, fallacious, or just plain stupid. For instance, one book developed by the Carnegie-Mellon Social Studies Curriculum Center follows a quote from President William McKinley's views on the American duty to Christianize the Philippines with these questions: "Does religious duty ever require that you impose benefits on other people if they do not want you to? Why do you feel as you do?"[101] The authors pose these curious questions without pointing out that Filipinos had been converted to Christianity several centuries before and McKinley was talking through his hat. In addition, some of the inquiry texts are quite as moralistic as any of their predecessors. The Carnegie-Mellon authors, for instance, go on from the above questions to ask, "Was it fair of [Albert] Beveridge and other Americans to consider commercial advantages to the United States when deciding whether to annex the Philippines?" The question supposes that when one country annexes another the only motive that might not be cricket is an economic one. The form of the inquiry text permits authors to avoid what they choose to, and some of them avoid the main issues. *The People Make a Nation*, by Martin W. Sandler, Edwin C. Rozwenc, and Edward C. Martin, evades all the issues of the Vietnam War by narrating the decisions taken to extricate American troops; the title of that section, "The Decision to Risk a Compromise Peace in Vietnam," is, of course, a misnomer, since that risk was never taken.

The inquiry texts also have failings that are specific to the form. Some of them, for instance, print the speeches of two parties to an argument without giving any background information on the issue or warning students that one or both parties may have been wrong or lying about the facts of the matter. History then becomes a mere matter of opinion — a high-school debate, in which what counts is not the merits of the case but the skill of the debaters. And here the choice of debaters is crucial. To pick an extremely bad example, one book purporting to examine the Cold War by analyzing the Korean War and the Suez crisis does nothing but quote speeches by President Harry S. Truman and President Dwight D. Eisenhower in defense of American policy.[102] Some of the inquiry texts — and chapters in most of them — take up subjects they don't have the space to treat properly and then ask questions that cannot be answered, or can be answered only improperly because of the paucity of information. Allan O. Kownslar and Donald B. Frizzle's *Discovering American History* — generally one of the better texts — asks students to "form a hypothesis" about the causes of the American Revolution on the basis of a few pages of introductory comments, the text of the Declaration of Independence, a fictional account of Thomas Jefferson's role in writing it, and a few paragraphs from an account of the writing of the Declaration by John Adams. Some of the texts cover up the poverty of their historical materials with a great deal of social-science jargon. And the thicker the jargon, the greater seems to be the incidence of loaded questions and loaded analogies. The Carnegie-Mellon book — its text awash with "concepts" — begins its section on "America and the World" in the twentieth century with the story of how Catherine Genovese was killed in a New York parking lot while numbers of people looked on from a nearby apartment house and did nothing. The text asks the student to think about "when you should help someone else" and "whether you should ever fight to help another person." It then goes on to discuss the Cold War, American aid programs, and American intervention in Vietnam. The message is unambiguous.[103]

Anyone of a generous disposition would be inclined to dismiss textbook philosophy as a somewhat random affair — the spontaneously generated product of the chaos of market forces, political pressures, individual quirks, and sheer carelessness: a salamander from the ooze. But this is not really the case. Ethnic and other interest groups do influence the specific political content of texts — they often demand an evasiveness that will protect group sensibilities — and fortuity in the shape of textbook editors determines many of the details. But textbook philosophy is a conscious creation; it is the work of people whose profession it is to think about the content of American education — school administrators, professors at teachers' colleges, curriculum-development experts, schoolteachers, and bureaucrats in federal and state offices of education. It is the product of committee meetings and debates in school journals, and it is no light matter. The development of the inquiry "concept" took thousands of man-hours and hundreds of thousands of dollars in federal funds — and even then it was not generally accepted. As for the philosophy of the older-style narrative texts, it was, and to a great degree remains, the philosophy of the secondary-school establishment.

At first glance, the educators and administrators who run the secondary-school system across the country — including the Florida State Text Committee and the members of the New York City Board of Education — would seem too vast and too disparate a collection of people to act as an establishment. Yet they do make up a system, and a fairly coherent one at that. American educationists (that is, the professionals who deal with education policy) have a common language — an arcane tongue barely comprehensible to outsiders — common concerns, and a high degree of national self-awareness. They have national organizations and professional journals and a common education in the teachers' colleges and schools of education. Fads and fashions, as well as long-term commitments, tend to sweep over the majority. At the moment, the school establishment is divided on a number of issues. But from about 1910 to the early sixties it held a fairly stable consensus on a philosophy of education and the way to teach children about the world and American history. The consensus originated in a series of policy statements by committees of the National Education Association and other curriculum-study groups early in the century. Among other things, these statements show how and why American-history texts came to be so dull.

According to educational historians, one of the most influential of all educational documents in the twentieth century is the 1918 report of the National Education Association on "Cardinal Principles of Secondary Education." As the main objectives of education in the secondary schools this report listed seven points: "health, command of fundamental processes [by which it meant the three Rs], worthy home membership, vocation, citizenship, worthy use of leisure, ethical character." It made no mention at all of the development of intellectual capacity or the mastery of academic subjects. Indeed, it made reference to a previous N.E.A. report that specifically repudiated these activities. This report, the 1911 report of the Committee of Nine on the Articulation of High School and College, had stated that the task of the high school was "to lay the foundations of good citizenship and to help in the wise choice of a vocation." It said, further, that the "bookish curricula" of the high schools had been responsible for "leading tens of thousands of boys and girls away from the pursuits for which they are adapted" to pursuits for which they are not, and giving them "false ideals of culture." It talked about "individual usefulness" and urged a much greater attention to vocational preparation. On the teaching of subjects such as history, geography, and economics, another N.E.A. committee report proposed in 1917 that the various disciplines be replaced by an integrated system of "social studies," in which the emphasis would shift from history to the social sciences and from the past to the present and the future. History, that committee wrote, "must relate to the present interests of the pupil, or meet the needs of present growth, in addition to explaining present-day conditions and institutions according to the sociological interpretation." The term "social studies," which had been given currency a few years earlier by an official of the United States Bureau of Education, implied at the time a commitment to social action — as the committee put it in a strong, restrictive negative, "Facts, conditions, theories and activities [that fail] to contribute rather directly to the appreciation of methods of human betterment [have] no claim." The committee therefore favored recent over ancient history, American history over that of "foreign lands," and "the labors and plans [of the multitudes] rather than the pleasures and dreams of the few." Instruction in the social studies, the report continued, "should be organized around concrete problems of vital importance to society and of immediate interest to the pupil," for the sake of increasing the "social efficiency" of students and helping them to "participate effectively in the promotion of social well-being."[104]

These documents were extraordinary, in that they contradicted the recommendations made by the N.E.A. two decades before. In the eighteen-nineties, at the time of the organization of the learned societies, a number of educational and academic groups, including the N.E.A., had taken a look at the disparate curricula of the high schools sprouting up across the country and — for the first time in American history — made an attempt to set national goals and national standards for the secondary schools. The reports they issued criticized the high schools both for their lack of attention to academic subjects and for the intellectual inadequacy of their teaching. In a manifesto typical of the period, the N.E.A.'s Committee on Secondary School Studies, usually known as the Committee of Ten, laid out recommendations for a rigorous academic program for the schools which gave particular emphasis to the teaching of history. The purpose of all education, the report said, was to train the mind; history was particularly important in this regard, because it cultivated the student's powers of judgment. The study of history, it stated, should be a laboratory science, a grappling with life.

In his *Anti-Intellectualism in American Life*, Richard Hofstadter shows that the abandonment of this philosophy of education and the substitution of a very different set of guiding principles (early in the nineteen-hundreds) coincided with a change in the leadership of the N.E.A. In the eighteen-nineties, college presidents and professors and headmasters of the élite private academies had more or less dominated the N.E.A. committees. But by the end of the eighteen-nineties the accelerating growth of the high-school population had brought the number of high-school teachers and administrators to a critical mass. Following the example of the university professors, the teachers organized their own, subject-related associations; they formed their own teacher-training colleges outside the regular university systems; and they took control of the secondary-school associations that existed. By 1910, the teachers and administrators had taken over the N.E.A. committees from the professors. The chairman of the 1893 Committee of Ten was, for example, Charles William Eliot, the president of Harvard; the chairmen of the later committees were, typically, teachers at manual-training high schools.[105]

The content of the new series of N.E.A. reports had, Hofstadter shows, a great deal to do with the background of the people who wrote them. The teachers in the common (or elementary) schools of the nineteenth century had always been poorly paid and minimally educated. And when the system of public secondary schools expanded, so, too, were the mass of new teachers. Toward the end of the century, those concerned with the curricula of the high schools began to adopt a utilitarian philosophy. Administrators and teachers put increasing faith in the notion that vocational training was the democratic alternative to the academic élitism of the European secondary schools. The idea that academic education might be made universal and therefore democratic had very little appeal — and not unnaturally since the high-school teachers would have been incapable of putting it into practice. The ideology of the teachers, however, merely reflected the fact that the community at large had no interest in providing intellectual training for the mass of high-school students; its concern was to train skilled workers for industry.

The academics who tried to raise the academic standards of the high schools in the 1890s had, as it happened, picked one of the worst moments to make the effort. That decade was a midpoint in the flood of new immigration from Europe. The public schools had always served as *the* public agencies for the acculturation of immigrants, and even with millions of new arrivals the city and state governments continued to repose the entire burden on them. Of necessity, the city schools became generalized social-welfare agencies, offering courses in English, home economics, and health care to adults as well as children. The educationists thus had some reason to assume that the goal of secondary education was health, vocational training, and citizenship training rather than academic studies.

Still, the educational philosophy introduced in the early nineteen-hundreds in reaction to the efforts of the academic reformers of the eighteen-nineties was utilitarian in ways that were neither traditional nor a matter of immediate practical necessity. The notion of the importance of the present relative to the past and the idea that education could and should be used for social reform came from the new — and still developing — ideology of the reform movement that centered on Theodore Roosevelt's Progressive Party. That movement, which encompassed a variety of reform efforts, from women's rights to work on behalf of immigrants, addressed not only political questions but also the wider issues of American culture. Indeed, it was, perhaps more than anything else, a cultural revolution. The goal of the progressives was not just to purge society of corruption but to liberate it from the dominion of the past — to put an end to respect for established tradition and to the Victorian culture of filial piety, authoritarianism, and class distinction. Like the Chinese in more modern times, the progressives believed that social action proceeded from education and a change in consciousness. Hugely impatient, hugely optimistic, they believed society could pull itself up by its own bootstraps.

In the field of education, there were two major trains of progressive thought: one concerned the individual and questions of artistic and psychological liberation; the other concerned society at large and the means of achieving a true democracy in an industrial era. Both came, of course, from John Dewey, but they were united only in the work of the master. For Dewey, culture was politics and vice versa; thus, one kind of liberation necessarily implied the other: the democratic society had to be founded on the democratic personality, and the New Man required a new society for his survival. Dewey's disciples created a series of new teaching methods and programs, loosely known as progressive education, and put them into practice in a number of public and private schools. But the progressive-education movement, never completely cohesive, split Dewey's philosophical coin in half. One group, descending into Greenwich Village, took up bohemian cultural criticism and experimentation with non-authoritarian teaching methods. The second group, composed of people such as George S. Counts and Harold Rugg, both professors at Columbia University's Teachers College, focussed on the problems of mass education and curriculum reform, with the aim of making the schools more democratic and better attuned to industrial society. Though they were far less radical, the educationists of the N.E.A. initially had more in common with the second group, for they tended to see art and psychology as the two compartments of Pandora's box. Eventually, however, they accepted some of the teachings of the first group in a much watered-down version. The task of assimilation was not really so great, for what the two groups had in common was their lack of interest in — or their actual hostility to — the academic disciplines and the notion of intellectual training.

Hofstadter has argued that John Dewey himself bears some responsibility for the anti-intellectual bent of American education. With regard to the teaching of history, there is certainly enough in Dewey's many and various works to support this thesis. Dewey's great enemy was intellectual conformity, and yet there is something reductive about his insistence on the utility of education to the child and the relevance of it to the child's interests. Then, too, there is an element in Dewey's philosophy which corresponds to the view held by certain painters in the nineteen-sixties that all museums ought to be burned. In "Democracy and Education," Dewey wrote:

> A knowledge of the past and its heritage is of great significance when it enters into the present, but not otherwise. And the mistake of making the records and remains of the past the main material of education is that it cuts the vital connection of present and past, and tends to make the past a rival of the present and the present a more or less futile imitation of the past. Under such circumstances, culture becomes an ornament and solace; a refuge and an asylum.[106]

Whatever Dewey really meant by his emphasis on relevance in history teaching, the N.E.A. educationists chose to take the narrowest possible view of it. While the bohemian progressives rejected historical training as but another way to repress the glorious clouds of imagination which children were born trailing, the N.E.A. committee members rejected history as trivia — as the games or ornaments of the élite. Under the noble standards of usefulness, they turned American history into civics and civics into propaganda for their version of the social good. For the dictatorship of the past they substituted that of the present, and for the flower child of the progressive-education movement they substituted the child immigrant to be "Americanized" by catechism.*

* See Cremin, *The Transformation of the Schools* (1961), for the history of progressive education and how the movement finally faded away.

The N.E.A. progressives did not reorder the curriculum of the public high schools overnight. Educational reform proceeds glacially in this country, with the result that the history texts in use from about 1910 through the twenties are a very mixed lot. Some of those written by distinguished professors show the influence of the academic reformers of the eighteen-nineties on the publishers. Some are polemical Progressive histories, and others are the work of New England ancestor worshippers. The upheavals of the Progressive era may have made the schools more open to novelties than usual. But by about 1930 the writ of the N.E.A. had run through the schools, leaving most of them with a course in American history and another in "problems of democracy," within a social-studies program, and setting the mold for textbooks. Harold Rugg's social-studies series for elementary- and junior-high-school students, published in the nineteen-thirties and forties, was in many ways the crowning achievement of the progressive-education movement in the field of textbooks, for, appearing in a new reformist period, it was, in fact, a democratic history — a history of the common man. It was also a work of persuasion, a conscious attempt to promote democratic values — particularly racial tolerance and an active commitment to social justice and equality of opportunity. In making his portrait of society, Rugg did not spare the warts but — and this showed that he was anything but a Marxist — pictured history merely as the constant striving of the well-intentioned common man to achieve a perfect democracy. What else had happened in history the books did not say — nor did they picture the common man of the seventeen-eighties as being any different from the common man of the nineteen-thirties. The series did not survive long enough to become old-fashioned, for in the nineteen-forties the textbook market took a sharp rightward turn, and it continued in that direction for the next twenty years. The enduring gift of the N.E.A. progressives to American-history teaching and to education in general was thus not their political idealism but their cultural narrowness.

To look back over the texts or the educational-policy statements of the nineteen-fifties is to see a piece of cultural syncretism quite as surprising as the Cargo Cults. On the one hand, all the policy statements reaffirm the primacy of the seven cardinal principles of secondary education laid down in 1918. A report published in the late nineteen-fifties by the National Council for the Social Studies, for instance, maintains, "There is a growing consensus that the schools should assume a primary responsibility for basic functions of education which were once almost entirely performed by family and church. These include moral and spiritual education, character education, education for home and family living, and other aspects of personal and social adjustment." In matters of civics, the report speaks in wholly Progressive terms about the need for the "vitalization of our democracy" and the "intelligent acceptance by individuals and groups of responsibility for achieving democratic social action." On the other hand, the political theme it proposes for social-studies courses is "Achieving a Balance Between Social Stability and Social Change" — and under that heading it remarks, "Political action generally involves a compromise between liberal and conservative forces." Elsewhere, it makes the utterly dogmatic assertion that "the egalitarian aim of abolishing social classes appears to be unrealistic. . . . The American pattern of social classification with a considerable social mobility offers the best discernible way of sharing power in the interest of justice." And, "Sturdy self-reliance coupled with an altruistic individualism is man's best hope."[107] The educationists had, in other words, managed to put the reformist curriculum of the Progressive era to work for conservative purposes; they had created a utopia of the present.

The interesting thing was, of course, that the conservatives who ruled the educational committees and school boards in the fifties had no more concern for academic education than the N.E.A. reformers in the first quarter of the century. The old academic curriculum had been declining for more than forty years. Latin, Greek, and ancient history had all but disappeared from the school curriculum; they were not replaced, for math, modern languages, European history, and science also had gone into a considerable decline — these bookish subjects giving way before the Alexandrianisms of baton-twirling, bayonet-twirling, and popularity contests. After the Second World War, the bohemian-progressive concerns for child development entered the public schools, in the much altered form of demands that children be "well-rounded personalities" — "creative," "spontaneous," and "well adjusted to the group." As Jacques Barzun noted at the time, the educationists had managed to invert the whole purpose of schooling, by assuming in each pupil "the supremely gifted mind, which must not be tampered with, and the defective personality, which the school must remodel."[108]

The American-history course survived mainly because it was required by state governments as part of civics training. But conservative politics did not imply any real interest in history. On the contrary, in the texts this was the period of maximum ahistoricism — the presentation of American democracy as a Platonic form abstracted from history. What appeared to be a purely political matter thus had serious pedagogical consequences. The Progressive texts had at least pointed out injustices and proposed alternatives, thereby leaving the student a little room for thought and questioning. The nineteen-fifties texts proposed a legalistic fiction that allowed for neither and that, incidentally, looked very much like the Progressive prescription for the society turned into a description of what was. The past was forgotten and the future became indistinguishable from the present. In that confusion of tenses, the United States was perfect and yet making progress all the time.

In the nineteen-fifties and sixties, the intrepid Henry Steele Commager published a series of essays complaining about the thinness of the academic curriculum in the high schools and the philistine attitudes toward culture in general and American history in particular. Attacking the goals of high-school history teaching, he wrote, "There is no reason to suppose that the compulsory study of American history at various levels in the elementary school and again in the high school necessarily makes good citizens."[109] His contention was heavily supported by a number of subsequent studies showing that in spite of all the investment in them, American-history, civics, and government courses did not influence students' attitudes appreciably or even leave them with very much information about the American government. The question is, however, whether the real aim of the state legislatures and school boards in requiring such courses was to increase students' knowledge of history and government—it was the professed aim. Throughout history, the managers of states have with remarkable consistency defined good citizenship as a rather small degree of knowledge of and participation in state affairs. The fury of college students in the sixties came in part from their sense that, along with government officials, their textbooks and their teachers had concealed from them the truth about American politics and history.

Complaining about the lack of academic rigor in schools was a fairly popular enterprise in the fifties, in spite of, or perhaps because of, the fact that it had all the risks and rewards of pillow-punching. The educationists were wholly caught up in questions of pedagogy. They studied children and designed batteries of tests to show the superior virtues of traditional or progressive teaching methods. The battles were Byzantine, for the tests, if they were at all objective, showed with unfailing regularity that it made hardly any difference which method was used: well-educated parents tended to insist on well-educated teachers and to have well-educated children, and that was that. Very few college professors took any interest in the subject of secondary education. University people had their own battles to fight on the ramparts of academic freedom, and those who bothered to consider a reform of the high schools usually took one look at the denizens of the teachers' colleges and declared the enterprise hopeless. The intellectual gap between high-school and college educators seemed unbridgeable, until Sputnik.

Sputnik was to American secondary education what the supposed "missile gap" of the early Kennedy era was to the military-industrial complex. The appearance of the Soviet satellite, in 1957, created a kind of panic in the United States. Received as a mysterious omen, Sputnik tipped the scales in favor of those who, like Admiral Hyman G. Rickover, sought to persuade significant numbers of Americans that the United States was falling behind, and not only in the space race but in science, technology, and education in general. Unfounded as this belief certainly was, the competitive instincts it aroused did what no amount of criticism in principle had been able to do. Overnight, the whole atmosphere changed. Congressmen called for a reëxamination of national priorities and an overhaul of the educational system. Teachers discovered that Johnny couldn't read, whereas Ivan could. Scientists found "shortages" of scientists, engineers, and mathematicians in the generations to come. Those scientists who all during the fifties had been complaining without being heeded were now heard to say that most secondary-school students were learning pre-Darwinian biology, pre-Einsteinian physics, and nineteenth-century math. The federal Office of Education and the National Science Foundation were given funds for extensive grants to the learned societies and the universities for the creation of new teaching materials and teacher-training programs in the sciences. And, unique in the annals of educational reform, these efforts had concrete and relatively speedy results.

About five years after Sputnik, this academic-reform movement reached the social studies. The delay was occasioned by the fact that it was much harder to find a utilitarian justification for reform of the social studies. The reformers eventually surmounted this barrier by complaining of the neglect of the social sciences and emphasizing the word "sciences." Congress finally could not object nor the high schools offer any real resistance to developing textbooks and courses in such well-established fields as economics, anthropology, political science, and so on. American history was trickier to deal with, since it was not even conceivably a science and since the state legislatures still required it as training for patriotism. Even more difficult was the whole field of social studies for younger children.

But the mid-sixties matched even the Progressive period in its optimism, and there was plenty of money around, so the reformers in the fields gained fairly large-scale support from the federal government.

Sputnik had precipitated all this activity, but there were important social forces behind the movement for educational reform. One of these was the growth of the college population after the Second World War. In 1939, four hundred and eighteen thousand students, or slightly more than a third of all high-school graduates, had gone on from secondary school to college; in the mid-sixties, one million two hundred and twenty-five thousand students, or more than half of all high-school graduates, were entering college. Academic credentials had always been seen as steps toward economic advancement, and with the increase in the national wealth over those two decades many more families could afford to send their children a step farther up that ladder. Also, in these two decades the shape of the American economy had changed; the new growth industries — services and government — required a larger number of people with certain intellectual skills. Critical thinking could no longer remain an aristocratic skill taught only in the best private schools, and since the high schools had proved incapable of teaching bright children these skills, the college system had to expand. Now, after spending twelve years memorizing and learning how to "identify with the group," a student could spend another four years learning how to reason. The college professors at the receiving end of this mass of uneducated eighteen-year-olds could less and less afford to ignore the intellectual inadequacies of the high schools.

A reform of the high schools, however, implied not just a change in curriculum but a change in the entire philosophy of primary- and secondary-school education. Of all the social-studies reformers, Jerome S. Bruner, who for many years was a developmental psychologist at Harvard, was the only one to take on the whole task. In answer to the educationists, Bruner proposed a new theory of pedagogy, the cardinal principle of which was that children at any stage in their development could be taught any subject in some intellectually honest form. Bruner, along with other reformers, inveighed against the criterion of relevance in the social studies and against the now traditional social-studies curriculum, which began in the first grade with the study of the home and worked outward in concentric — indeed, Confucian — circles to the community, the state, the nation, and the world. Children, Bruner argued, were not interested only in what was close to home or in the information that would be of practical use to them in later life. What attracted them was myth and drama. As for the banalities the educationists served up as the stuff of everyday life, these did not teach children how to think. Children could learn to generalize immediately, but they had to have a theoretical model, and the more exotic it was, the better. The fifth-grade social-studies program that Bruner inspired, called "Man: A Course of Study," showed children how to explore the most general questions about the nature of human beings by examining bird and primate groups and then the Netsilik Eskimos. For Bruner, math and poetry were the "metaskills" of the future.[110]

Among reformers in what became known as the New Social Studies movement, there was general agreement on Bruner's main tenets. Some of the reformers shared Bruner's ambition to create a "psychology" of the behavioral sciences, or a "grammar of learning," which would be the translation of epistemology into child psychology. What they meant by this was not completely clear, but presumably they wished to do for the social sciences what the New Math reformers were doing for mathematics. For others, the problem was simply to present the disciplines of the social sciences to children in an orderly and intellectually honest form. But even this enterprise was highly ambitious. High-school students could, of course, be taught economics or sociology with textbooks that were modified versions of the introductory materials used in college courses. But how to design an integrated program of social studies for the young? And how to teach history to any age group?

In the field of history, one of the leading strategists and advocates of the New Social Studies was Edwin Fenton, a professor of history and until last year the director of the Carnegie-Mellon University Social Studies Curriculum Center. In his book *The New Social Studies* and elsewhere, Fenton argued that the old-style texts and teaching methods had offered students merely a list of facts and weak generalizations they could not possibly retain. What students needed was a context for information and a way of dealing with it: they needed to know how to think. A successful social-studies program, Fenton said, would teach students the concepts of social science and certain basic analytical skills. As a method of teaching cognitive skills, Fenton proposed what he called the "mode of inquiry" — a process whereby the student would work from more or less raw data and the concepts of social science to draw his own conclusions. This was the basis for all the so-called inquiry, or discovery, textbooks. Fenton did not believe that students could duplicate the work of a historian on any given issue, but he thought that they could approximate the logical processes, with the help of carefully selected data and analytical questions. He proposed that teachers measure success not just by the quantity of information students digested but by the skills they acquired. Students should, he said, be taught "procedural values" — that is, attitudes of rational thought — but not "substantive values"; they should be taught merely how to analyze questions of substantive value.

Fenton's notion of "inquiry" teaching caught on among the reformers, and in the early sixties the federal Office of Education and the National Science Foundation funded several university groups, including Fenton's Carnegie-Mellon Center, to develop teaching materials in this mode. These groups took a variety of different approaches. Some concerned themselves principally with the abstract questions of which skills and concepts were most important to the social sciences and in what order they should be taught to children. Others occupied themselves with designing histories that would — they hoped — be of interest to children and of some academic value. Still others, such as Fenton, also became entrepreneurs of the New Social Studies, managing curriculum projects, writing articles, and lecturing teachers on the new pedagogical techniques.

The New Social Studies made rather heavy weather in the secondary-school establishment. In part, it was the contrast of styles. The reformers had a lot in common with the whiz-kid intellectuals in the John F. Kennedy Administration at the time. They were all energy, all ideas, all brash self-confidence. They did not know very much about the schools, but it seemed obvious to them that the system was backward and reactionary, and that, by contrast, they represented the modern world, where knowledge was power and the ability to think was the ability to control. Like the progressives in the early part of the century, they felt their criticisms to be self-evident and their reforms so long overdue that, given the support of the federal government, nothing could stand in their way. Most of them had a rather low opinion of schoolteachers and saw the retraining of them as an important part of their job. As might be expected, the teachers resented this attitude. Many of them did not look upon the New Social Studies as reasonable and self-evident. They looked upon the reformers as élitists — "the ivory-tower crowd" — who knew nothing about the practice of teaching children and who had ideas quite contrary to common sense. "I once met Jerome Bruner," a social-studies textbook editor and former teacher told me, "and I asked him, 'Why the Netsilik Eskimos?' And he answered, 'Why not?' " The editor thought the answer frivolous — as Bruner had no doubt thought the question foolish.

But the dichotomy between the two groups was not as precise as either imagined. Attacked for being too intellectual, the reformers were in fact not intellectual enough. Nearly all of them, even Bruner, lacked philosophical training. Not only did they fail to develop any original ideas about the structure of knowledge but they actually confused the social sciences with science. Some wasted a great deal of time making and unmaking meaningless conceptual schemes. Others, like Fenton in *The New Social Studies*, would explain a few elementary points of logic and then disappear into a cloud of pedagogical or social-science jargon. Finally, they did not do what really had to be done if the schools were to make any advances in the art of training minds — and that was to define new purposes and set new standards for the curriculum. The reformers came up with a few daring and original programs for younger children, notably Bruner's *Man: A Course of Study*. The academics who wrote new introductory texts in the social sciences did some very good work. Academic historians did not — interestingly enough — participate in the New Social Studies programs as much as academics from other disciplines did, with the result that some of the new histories were solid work and others were not at all.

Fenton's own curriculum project was, in fact, something of a disaster. The Social Studies Curriculum Center spent more than four years and three hundred and sixty-four thousand dollars in federal money developing a four-year high-school course on the social studies. After more than four years, the developers had not one piece of material in publishable form; no test, except one of their own devising, showed more than a marginal difference between the analytical abilities of the students who had taken their course and those of the students in the control group, which had followed the traditional curriculum. Partly because of Fenton's reputation in educational circles, Holt, Rinehart & Winston eventually published the course — but only after substantial revisions were made in the content of the books. (The curriculum developers had not, it turned out, sent the manuscripts to any outside academic authorities in the fields they covered, from Soviet economics to American history.) However, the form of the books went largely unchanged — and the form is disturbing. Far from being rigorous examples of the inquiry mode, the history books contain long, tendentious essays in every section and lists of tendentious questions that more or less predetermine value judgments. (There are also questions, such as the one about McKinley Christianizing the Filipinos, that are completely illogical.) The books are not wholly without merit — they contain a number of interesting readings — but they hardly justify Fenton's pedagogical fuss about a "closely coordinated and sequential set of learning experiences," nor do they insure that the student will become "an informed, responsible citizen of a democratic society" any better than do the traditional narrative histories.

One notable thing about the reformers was that, Bruner aside, they could not seem to deal with the implications of the New Social Studies. The inquiry method, after all, implied a philosophy of education very different from the now traditional utilitarian doctrines; it implied a far broader view of culture, a less reductive child psychology, and an agnostic attitude toward life in general. The reformers did not attack on these grounds; in defending the New Social Studies, they chose the far narrower (and more questionable) terrain of the importance of social science and the usefulness of their procedures to learning abilities. The narrowness of their outlook was particularly remarkable when they came to rationalize the teaching of American history. Allan O. Kownslar, for example, a leading New Social Studies advocate and the author of several inquiry texts in American history, made the argument in one education yearbook that American history should be taught because historians were now making greater use of social-science concepts. (The typical foreword to the New Social Studies texts states that history should be studied because it is "the best laboratory for testing social-science concepts.")[111] After staggering about in search of such a justification-by-social-science, most of the reformers would come reeling back to the old lamppost of citizenship training. Fenton, indeed, never left that post. In *The New Social Studies*, he argued that critical thinking would be of help in achieving the traditional goal of the social studies —

citizenship. He never defined citizenship, nor did he resolve the contradiction between citizenship training and his strictures against the teaching of "substantive values." In general, the New Social Studies people seemed to regard scientific thinking as merely a tactic for traditional utilitarian ends. Even Bruner justified his pure-math, pure-poetry position on the ground that these "metaskills" would be necessary for the control of technology in the future.

That the one school-reform movement in this century led by academics should have taken such a narrow, specialized form was not perhaps surprising, given what was happening at the universities during the same period. For the universities were exploding. Not only were they experiencing an unprecedented growth in undergraduate enrollments, they were finding new sources of revenue in government and industry and were building new professional schools, research institutes, and laboratories. One consequence of this growth was a fragmentation of the undergraduate curriculum. The notion of a liberal education fell from favor — it came to be regarded as a playground for amateurs and gentlemen. The new wealth of the universities brought not only a change in structure but a change in over-all purpose and philosophy. As the universities expanded, they outgrew their purely academic functions to become training grounds for industry and government. The college presidents who in the fifties had so righteously defended the principle of intellectual freedom from McCarthyite attacks now accepted government research grants on the principle that the universities should be of some service to government and industry. Infiltration had worked where frontal attack had not, and the ivory towers were not destroyed but overwhelmed. Students went to college in order to qualify for managerial jobs, and a significant number of professors in the natural and social sciences left academic life without ever leaving the universities. These professors did not see themselves as bought or hired; they subscribed to the new theories about the "technetronic" or "post-industrial" society which promised that intellectuals would end up controlling the state by virtue of their expertise. (These theories of Zbigniew Brzezinski, Daniel Bell, and others are now included in many secondary-school texts; the educationists look on them with favor, since they certify the utility of education and the democracy of the American system.) Whether or not the prediction was correct, the academics involved in state business were involved in something other than pure science or the expansion of knowledge for its own sake. The academic school reformers of the early sixties thus stood at a point of convergence between the university and secondary-school establishments. The convergence had occurred not because of a change of philosophy in the schools but because in the fifties and sixties the universities had in many respects taken over the purposes and the former role of the secondary schools. This convergence had the effect of making the reformers far more acceptable to educationists and high-school teachers than they ever were before. Now the educationists could look upon the intellectual life as having some practical value. They could look upon at least some professors as respectable, useful citizens. They could accept the New Math, modern science, and the New Social Studies as new forms of vocational training.

The New Social Studies did not sweep away the old, as so many of its advocates confidently supposed that it would. The inquiry texts now cover only about fifteen per cent of the market, and the National Science Foundation programs — *Man: A Course of Study* and the like — have reached only a small minority of schools. (According to the publisher, as of 1974 "MACOS" had been sold to only seventeen hundred schools out of fifty-eight thousand public and private elementary schools in the nation.) The ten best-selling American-history texts are still very much in the old progressive civics-as-history mold. The New Social Studies has had some influence on them. These and other narrative texts include flourishes of social-science "concepts" and very often sections in which social scientists argue the causes of the Great Depression or explain the concept of "role." In a few of the books for younger children published in the late sixties, social scientists are presented as role models for children. On the other hand, a number of the newer inquiry books have been watered down pedagogically, their documentary sections cut with narrative text that "covers" the usual sequence of events.

The reformers might have anticipated passive resistance from the secondary-school teachers. The public-school system is, after all, one of the most conservative of American institutions; it has a protoplasmic quality that combines a superficial sensitivity with a profound resistance to change. Many teachers objected to the gimmickry of the New Social Studies, while others remained unconvinced of the need for more intellectual training. What the reformers could not have anticipated was the philosophic reaction that came from outside the educational establishment proper. The reaction came in two waves — first from the youth movements of the sixties and then, during the Nixon years, from the cultural fundamentalists.

At just about the time the New Social Studies had gained some acceptance in the educational establishment, a new group of educational critics began to attack it in much the same terms as their counterparts in the foreign-policy debate used to attack Robert McNamara. In their view — as one historian put it — the real failure of American education was not its mindlessness but its heartlessness. For these new critics, the training of the intellect was a narrow pursuit; education, in their view, was a search for personal fulfillment and the means of reforming society. The purpose of education was to create understanding, feeling human beings — not technocrats with computers for brains. A number of these critics stressed notions of "authenticity" and personal liberation. This "greening," or counterculture, school argued that training in the academic disciplines developed a specialized, compartmentalized mind, out of touch with the emotions and therefore tending to become a mere servant to a runaway technology that destroyed nature and the natural. The politically inclined critics — those aligned with the civil-rights and antiwar movements — saw academic training as specifically élitist. Pretending to universality, it was really a product of a white, middle-class culture which inevitably doomed minority students to failure and confirmed white, middle-class children in their complacent irresponsibility. While the first group focussed on the role of the teacher and what happened in the classroom, the second emphasized the curriculum, advocating the replacement of academic courses with "problems" courses that would broach subjects of immediate social concern and lead to a greater sense of social responsibility. In their nearly limitless expectations of what the schools could do, the new critics were well within the American tradition; indeed, they were the lineal descendants of John Dewey and the two schools of the progressive-education movement.

By about 1970, these new critics could point to some changes in the direction of educational policy. In the first place, they had persuaded both federal and local agencies of the need to give special attention to the education of "disadvantaged" children — particularly to minority-group children of the inner cities. With respect to teaching materials, the result was that these agencies took the balance of their funds away from New Social Studies projects and other programs for advanced students and gave it to projects such as Head Start, *Sesame Street*, and books for "slow learners." In the second place — and at least partly in response to the new critics — the content of the social-studies curriculum changed appreciably. In schools across the country, "problems" courses replaced courses teaching the social sciences as disciplines. Subjects of current concern — youth studies, black studies, and the Vietnam War — invaded the schoolbooks and the classrooms, driving out slightly less modern history. Along with this concern for "problems" came a new pedagogical fad for "values clarification" — meaning a conscious attempt to teach teachers how to teach students to define their own values. The political passions of the sixties died out in short order, but the "problems" approach and the emphasis on social action lived on, thus bringing the wheel of social-studies reform full circle.[112]

The right-wing reaction followed fairly closely on the heels of the sixties, and it struck most heavily at the one link between the New Social Studies and the neo-progressive reformers — that is, at what the right saw as their implicit moral and cultural relativism. Incidents of book burning and demonstrations over the content of school courses took place across the country, some of them in New England and the Middle West in communities of educated, middle-class people. In Washington, Representative John B. Conlan, of Arizona, led a crusade against "MACOS" and other National Science Foundation projects, with the support of right-wing groups.

Some of these demonstrations and book-burning incidents could be construed merely as conservative protests against the more alarming cultural novelties of the sixties — with under-currents of racism. There was a good deal of free-floating indignation about the anti-war movement, Black Power, sexual permissiveness, and so forth — and the leaders of the movement played heavily on it. (And often hypocritically. The National Science Foundation received letters from various parts of the country complaining that "MACOS" advocated polygamy and wife-swapping. Since Netsilik sexual customs had been mentioned only in the teacher's guide, the charge was nonsense, and the repetition of it suggested that some organization was waging a deliberate campaign of slander.) For some, however, there was a great deal more involved — in fact, an entire philosophy basically at odds with political liberalism, cultural modernism, and the spirit of scientific inquiry. The most surprising part of this new movement was the reappearance of the creationist argument fifty years after the Scopes trial. In California, the Board of Education issued guidelines for the state's biology curriculum which included the statement that the Book of Genesis presents a reasonable explanation for the origin of life and the recommendation that the concept of special creation be taught as an alternative to the concept of evolution.

Right behind this fundamentalist upsurge came a wave of reaction against the pedagogical liberalism of the sixties: the so-called Back to Basics movement. Different in kind from its predecessor, this movement was more or less a ground swell that moved across the nation, and it was, in some sense, truly conservative. The Back to Basics argument had several layers to it. At bottom was the simple, and in the end quite generally accepted, proposition that because reading and math scores were declining nationwide the schools had better pay more attention to teaching the three Rs. On top of that, there were various arguments about the cause of this decline and the remedy for it. Some critics blamed the looseness of the curriculum, with all its fancy new elective courses; others blamed progressive teaching methods, such as the open classroom; and others blamed the New Math and the New Social Studies. A fair number blamed all of the above, arguing that the best approach was still the old one of drill work and grading. The moderates among these Back to Basics critics seemed merely to want to clear away some of the undergrowth of electives, mini-courses, and non-academic work from the school curriculum. The extremists seemed to be insisting that rote work was in some metaphysical way good for children or that schoolwork should not be any more interesting than that which they themselves had endured.

By the mid-seventies, the influence of both the fundamentalists and the Back to Basics people began to show up in the texts — as well as in certain school systems. After the California guidelines were issued, the publishers began to revise their biology texts; while they did not insert passages from the Book of Genesis, they modified statements on evolution so as to leave certain ambiguities. (These modifications did not, apparently, lower the academic quality of the texts; scientists say the new versions are more accurate.) The fundamentalists also forced revisions of a number of literary anthologies that contained offending passages about white racism, the evils of the war in Vietnam, and words as standard in the English language as "damn." (Because at the same time blacks, Mexican-Americans, women, and others were pressuring the publishers to include works by minority-group members, the books now include works by blacks, women, etc., which do not mention the issues that concern these groups the most.) In a period of economic downturn, pressure from both the fundamentalists and the conservatives curtailed experimental programs of all sorts in the social-studies field. Federal funding for the development of new teaching materials declined; in just one year, the sales of "MACOS" dropped by seventy per cent; the inquiry texts were modified; and the narrative-style histories increased in popularity.

The neo-progressives of the nineteen-sixties, the fundamentalists, and the Back to Basics people all had a powerful influence on the inner establishment of professional educationists — that is, the school administrators, the state bureaucrats, the curriculum developers, and so on. The growth of that influence could be measured by the progress of the debate in the education journals. For a brief period in the early sixties, the educationists writing in those journals had laid moral issues aside to focus on the intellectual problems of social-studies teaching. By the mid-sixties, they were back to discussing moral issues again — but very much within the framework of the New Social Studies. In a book called "Inquiry in Social Studies," published in 1966, two prominent educationists, Byron G. Massialas and C. Benjamin Cox, made an extended case for Fenton's position against teaching "substantive values." The society, they said, was so pluralistic and so divided and confused over questions of value that the only thing a social-studies teacher could hope to do was to raise the level of debate. Their rather radical conclusion was that "education can no longer play only the role of culture preserver, mediator, or innovator but must make its most important contribution within the area of intelligent choice and decision on the part of the individual."[113] In other words, the schools should make it their primary business to teach children how to think. The agnosticism of Massialas and Cox — it is worthy of note — was based not on the morality of science but, rather, on an analysis of American society. And throughout the sixties most prominent educationists made a similar analysis — that the society was fundamentally divided. By the early seventies, the educational theorists had not only lost interest in improving the intellectual quality of education for its own sake but had ceased to mention intellectual skills — even in the context of improving civics instruction. The social-studies journals were filled with discussions of the methods teachers should use to get students to define their own values. This enthusiasm for "values clarification" was succeeded by an enthusiasm for "the development of decision-making skills." In a yearbook of the National Council for the Social Studies, one high-school "social-studies chairperson" proposed that, to enhance their decision-making, students should not only study problems, such as the world food crisis, but find solutions to them and send them on to their congresspersons. He also suggested that teachers ask students to "role play," by giving them such problems as: What would you do if in 1942 your best friend was being taken away to an internment camp for Japanese-Americans? Or: What would you say to Nixon if you were his aide and you discovered the coverup in the winter of 1973?[114] The old civics approach was back again.

By the mid-seventies, even the former leaders of the New Social Studies movement had come around to the view that teaching values was important. In 1974, Allan O. Kownslar, the editor of several inquiry texts, was defending the teaching of American history on the ground that it could "lend itself naturally to a developmental interplay between objectives within the cognitive and affective domains"[115] — or, in other words, that it could mold attitudes and feelings as well as teach skills. Edwin Fenton went further than this. Indeed, to a degree he repudiated the New Social Studies; he had, he said, exaggerated the ability of children to learn analytical skills and underestimated how much they needed training in thinking about moral problems. In the April, 1976, issue of *Social Education,* Fenton took on the role of publicist for the work of Lawrence Kohlberg, a Harvard professor of education, who for some years had been engaged in elaborating a universal theory of moral development. According to Fenton, Kohlberg had established six identifiable stages of moral development, ranging from consideration of imminent punishment to consideration of universal ethical principles. He had also, Fenton said, established that the higher stages were better than the lower ones and that people could be taught to rise from one stage to the next by reasoned examination of real or hypothetical moral conflicts. In the course of this exegesis, Fenton urged that teachers undertake to instruct their students in "cognitive moral development" by means of the Socratic dialogue.[116]

After this partial defection by one of its leading advocates, the New Social Studies was clearly dead. All that remained was for the new president of the National Council for the Social Studies, James P. Shaver, to write its epitaph. In his 1976 presidential address, Shaver said:

> For many years . . . social studies personnel were too busy with teaching "academic" content to pay much attention to values and valuing as part of citizenship education. In fact, the "structure of the discipline" approach that dominated most of the curriculum development projects which masqueraded as social studies projects in the 1960s was a fad that exemplified our long standing and unthinking subservience to professors in the academic disciplines.[117]

In the same address, Shaver questioned whether it was "justifiable . . . to expose all school children to all verified social science knowledge" and asked whether the schools should teach "MACOS" at the elementary level.

The educational debates of the nineteen-sixties and early seventies rivalled those of the Progressive era in scale and intensity. Because public discussions of how the next generation should be prepared for life reveal basic values and intellectual attitudes, these debates showed a good deal about the way Americans think and what they believe in. Taken together, what the debates suggest is that the real divisions in American society lie not between Republicans and Democrats or conservatives and liberals but among those groups one might call progressives, fundamentalists, and mandarins. These groups are not just political entities but whole cultures, as different from one another as the Zuñi and the Kwakiutl. The progressives are children of Rousseau, who believe in an egalitarian society, in the perfection of "nature," and in the perfectibility of man through education or a change in consciousness. The fundamentalists believe in God, not in man; they believe that man and society can survive only by the strictest obedience to a single, permanent set of truths, laws, and values. The mandarins are temperamental agnostics, who believe nonetheless in meritocracy, in the power of the intellect, and in the value of science and the cultural tradition. Over the years, these three groups have done battle with one another over almost every issue in education: who should control the schools, what should be taught in them, and whose interests should be served. In spite of their differences, however, they have, over the course of a century, come to adopt much the same attitude toward the purpose of schooling and the psychology of children.

The educational committees of the eighteen-nineties — the mandarins of that period — took it as an axiom that the purpose of the schools was to pass along the knowledge of one generation to the next, and in the most thorough and efficient way possible. Children could then do what they liked with it, including turning the whole thing over. The professors claimed no special authority except that of experience in their own subjects. They criticized the traditional public-school curriculum on the ground of its thinness, its poverty; they believed that schools could provide much richer fare for the minds of American children. More recently, however, the educational reform movements have veered in the opposite direction. Rather than try to broaden the flow of knowledge, they have tried to limit it to certain prescribed courses. What unites all recent educational movements is not just the narrow view they take of the culture but their manipulativeness with regard to children. It is this attitude that prevails among so many professional educationists and that makes the American-history textbooks so ahistorical and so boring.

In the education debates of the sixties and seventies, the progressive tendency has been represented by two groups — the New Romantics, as one historian called the counterculture critics of the sixties, and the political radicals. The

New Romantics declared that their goal was to make education larger and more generous; they called for free play, creativity, authenticity, direct experience, and joy. This program did not necessarily exclude intellectual development and intellectual creativity. But because the New Romantics saw the technocracy — intellectual and otherwise — as the main enemy, they tended to look upon all intellectual pursuits as narrow, "academic," and stunting to the psyche. Not considering themselves intellectuals — and some of them were, by training, just that — they manufactured a dichotomy between freedom, creativity, and pleasure on the one hand and rationality on the other. If only because of its iconoclasm, the counterculture movement had a rejuvenating influence on American culture in general, but because of its anti-intellectualism it had the opposite effect on the school curriculum. Like their forebears in the Progressive era, the New Romantics argued that education should be non-authoritarian and that children should be allowed to develop naturally, spontaneously. But, as Jacques Barzun, among others, pointed out, there is a difference between education and schooling. If the main purpose of schooling is to teach children subjects, then schools are by their nature undemocratic places — if only because teachers know more than children do about history and math. Those teachers who embraced the New Romantic ideology had the choice of concealing the authority they were in fact exerting or ceasing to teach subjects, in the interest of democracy. Those who were ideologically opposed to measuring students by their academic achievements had only the alternative of measuring them by their behavior and attitudes: Was the child creative and spontaneous? Teachers had to claim to be ultimate judges of personality, and, more than that, molders of character rather than experts (relative to children) in history or math.

As for the political radicals, they, too, were character molders, though in a different sense. When they described the horrors of urban-slum schools, they spoke as if these schools, properly run, could save children from the rest of society—and then change the world. They attacked the conservative content of the public-school curriculum, arguing that the new social-science courses were not much different from the old civics courses, in that they concealed more than they taught, and taught only acquiescence to the status quo. But then, after ridiculing fifties-style civics, they called for "relevant" courses in the *real* problems of democracy, to promote real social reform. The ease with which the schools adopted such courses should have been a warning to them, but it was not, and they were shocked when they discovered that their reforms had had an effect opposite to the one they desired.

In early 1976, Jonathan Kozol, an author and a former public-school teacher, wrote a fierce attack on the new generation of social-studies courses in an Op-Ed piece for *The New York Times*. Ironically, the attack was a perfect illustration of the difficulties inherent in the philosophy of the political radicals. Kozol wrote that he had interviewed students from a white suburban high school about a year-long research project they had done called "Urban Crisis and Race Turmoil in the Nineteen Sixties." The project had been advertised as "free" and "open," and it had taken children into the neighboring slums. But, according to Kozol, the children had reacted by putting an enormous distance between themselves and "the problem" out there. One child explained why. "We know," he said, "that . . . we're the ones who get the good end of the deal. . . . We talk about things we don't intend to change. Why change a situation which puts us right where we want, and other people . . . so far away we never even need to know that they exist?" What outraged Kozol was the cynicism these students had apparently learned. The school "research" courses, he concluded, were just as venal and corrupting as those carried on by the technocrats of the "good" colleges, where these students would soon go. Rather than promoting "*effective action*" (the italics are his), the schools were "turning out another generation of self-serving experts in the art of Needless Knowledge and Inert Ideas." He felt, he reported, a momentary rage on realizing this, but then he came around to a more realistic point of view. "Ethics? Action? Social transformation? What did I expect to find here in this modern, antiseptic, subdivided flagstone-decorated prison of the soul? What do we really think these schools are for?"[118]

The question really is, however, why Kozol supposed that such schools would promote his particular brand of effective action and social transformation. And then, if they did promote it, why he supposed that students would not see it as a barefaced attempt to manipulate them. From a left-wing point of view, it was naïve of Kozol to suppose that a school would not reflect the views of the community that paid for its services. And if he was proposing that schools should not reflect community views, then he had to answer a number of questions about the role of democratic institutions which he did not in fact address. His view of children was equally primitive. Apparently Kozol had believed that children could grow up to the age of seventeen without developing any sense of their own place in society. Or else he believed that classrooms full of children could be converted from the politics of their parents by one or two schoolteachers. In either case Kozol was dangerously underestimating the very people he had hoped would transform society: the schoolchild-revolutionaries he envisioned were babes in the wood.

To accuse the New Romantics or the political reformers of the sixties of philistinism would be to call forth countercharges of irrelevance or frivolity. But it is seldom that one finds such a perfect illustration of Santayana's thesis that those who do not learn history are bound to repeat it. The Progressive educationists of the 1910s had also believed in social reform through education, and they, too, had achieved a great deal in the way of turning public attention to the plight of children in the urban slums. But then, in part because they disapproved of what had happened in the past, they turned away from history altogether, refusing to admit it as a subject for study, assuming that it would somehow disappear behind them, like land behind an ocean-going vessel. But the future is a very insubstantial thing — a few hopes, a few plans, and otherwise vapors. Having launched themselves into this world without bearings, they found their own ship of social efficiency sailing in the opposite direction under the command of others. Painfully they figured out what had happened. In 1930 one of the best-known of the radical educationists, George S. Counts of Columbia Teachers College, did a study demonstrating that the high schools reflected the external social structure and perpetuated its values. He concluded that teachers could not hope to change society in any fundamental way — they could merely hope to humanize it. But the political radicals of the sixties had apparently never read this. The grandchildren of the Progressives, they had inherited their disdain for the past; while engaging in an act of filiopiety, they were quite unconscious of it.

What is interesting about both generations of Progressives is the convergence between their view of the culture and their view of child psychology. Their prescriptions for education are put most precisely as limitations on what can be taught: the N.E.A. committees of the Progressive era proposed to deny children all information that did not contribute to their social efficiency or "the appreciation of the modes of human betterment"; Kozol thought courses in "urban crisis" should not be taught except as spurs to social action. The psychology in both cases is monkey-see-monkey-do — except that it presumes that children only see what they are told to see in school. How the Progressives arrived at this pedagogical theory is mystifying until one examines fundamentalist pedagogy — at which point it becomes quite obvious that it is simply the fundamentalist position turned upside down.

In 1975 Representative John Conlan, then the leading congressional spokesman for the fundamentalist position, attacked Bruner's anthropology course, "MACOS," on the grounds that it was a "vehicle for behavior modification." Many people, he wrote, "blame Bruner for alcoholism, disregard for property rights, vandalism, uncivil behavior, epidemic VD, disdain for the work ethic, callousness, cynicism and belief in the occult."[119] The statement is, of course, startling. What it suggests is that the psyches of children are so frail that if the schools present them with any exception to what the community defines as correct behavior they will plunge into a moral abyss from which nothing can save them. Conversely, then, all education ought to consist solely of instruction in, or examples of, how adults think children ought to live. Children should be shown only correct behavior — even if this means concealing much of the world from them and lying about much of the rest of it. The argument is founded on a firm belief in the efficacy of "behavior modification." Thus, it is not, as it first appears, an argument against behavior modification but, on the contrary, an argument that it should be done, and done correctly.

After all the farfetched theories of the progressives and the fundamentalists, the Back to Basics argument appears at first glance to be the essence of sanity — a purgative for all the excessive rhetoric and a promise to return the schools to their task of schooling. Its central thesis is unarguable: children ought to come out of school knowing how to read, write, and do math, and not enough of them do, in spite of the fact that the school system soaks up ever-increasing amounts of the national wealth. But that is about that. For, beyond this solid axiom, the Back to Basics argument floats out past the reaches of evidence and logic into the sphere of mysticism.

In the August 28, 1977, issue of *The New York Times Magazine*, Frank E. Armbruster, of the Hudson Institute, performed the service of condensing the full Back to Basics argument into a few pages. He stated, first of all, that the ability of American children to read and write had declined over the past ten years; this decline, he said, was the result of the failure of the schools to educate children as well as they used to. For this failure he blamed school reformers and many of the innovations that had been made in the school system since the nineteen-thirties. In order of their appearance, his objections were: the New Social Studies reformers; English-as-a-second-language programs; "open-[ing] the schoolyard gate to the language, grammar, habits, dress and values of the slums"; democracy in the classroom;

the New Math; audiovisual programs; "modular scheduling," "open classrooms," and the elective curriculum; and laxness, permissiveness, and laziness on the part of teachers. Children must, he concluded, learn basic skills and basic information, and the only way to insure that they do is to throw out these innovations and go back to the old-fashioned system of rote work, grading, and drill.

The first problem with the argument is that there is no hard evidence for any of Armbruster's propositions. Several, though not all, indicators show that the ability to read and write has declined over the past ten years, but this recent decline is difficult to assess, given the change in the school population. That this decline is the fault of the schools is simply a guess, since — if the decline exists — there are so many other possible causes, such as the decline of parental discipline or the omnipresence of television. As for the contention that traditional methods are superior to all others, there is some evidence that this is nonsense. In the nineteen-forties, the last time the Back to Basics movement was riding high, a respectable group of educators did a test on college students to determine the effectiveness of progressive education; the test, which continued for eight years, showed that students who graduated from progressive schools had a slightly higher academic achievement in college than students who graduated from traditionally run schools.[120] This one test may not be proof positive — the variables in educational testing are nearly impossible to control — but in all the hundreds of studies done on children over the past few decades it has never been shown that children learn better by drill and rote methods than by any other system. The Back to Basics people may be right about certain of the innovations, but since they condemn opposite theories and forms of education in the same breath — nineteen-fifties-style "progressive education" *and* the New Math and Social Studies — they cannot show how or why, or even whether, they are right. The blanket indictment of all new methods makes for an implausible argument.

In fact, the Back to Basics argument is not a theory at all but, rather, a mood that sweeps the country from time to time. It is not even a specific reaction to progressive education, since it is far, far older than that. Complaints about the decline of education due to modern permissiveness go back at least to the mid-nineteenth century. As a national mood, it often coincides with the ends of wars and with periods of economic downturn. Conservative, pessimistic, nostalgic, it seems to be some kind of quest for certainty in an uncertain world. The argument itself is not racist or anti-democratic, but it always seems to appear in the wake of efforts to democratize the school system, and its proponents always insist on the importance of maintaining middle-class standards and values. It also contains an undertone of curmudgeonliness with regard to the young: they've had it easy, and now they've got to be disciplined, toughened up, the way we were. In its distrust of experimentalism and its glorification of the past, it is the opposite of what might be called the progressive temperament. At bottom, it is not conservative but fundamentalist, for its proponents, too, have no interest in history and no sense that the whole culture is worth preserving. Then, too, the Back to Basics theorists are clearly warning teachers against any ambitions they might have to teach critical thinking or the uses of the imagination. The "basics" are to them grammatical rules, facts, dates — also, instruction in patriotism and filiopiety.

Of all the educational movements of the sixties and seventies, only that of the academic reformers promised to liberate the philosophy of the schools from the reductive progressive-fundamentalist ideology. All the academic reformers — including Admiral Rickover — took the view that the purpose of schooling was to train the minds, not the characters, of children; they believed that the schools had a rather modest obligation toward society and that they were failing to fulfill it. A number of the people involved in the reform movement were heirs to the academics on the eighteen-nineties school committees in their belief that the schools could offer much richer intellectual fare across the board. This view was not, however, universal among the reformers, and it was not at all the view that percolated down through the ranks of the educationists into the school system.

One major difference between the two groups of academic reformers — the professors of the eighteen-nineties and the New Social Studies theorists of the nineteen-sixties — was that those of the sixties failed to create a new curriculum for the secondary schools. Apart from the impossible project of creating a "grammar of learning," the sixties theorists had no more comprehensive a program for the schools than the simple injunction to teach more (and more modern) science and social science. One reason for this lack of comprehensiveness was that many of the important figures in the movement represented special interests and special constituencies with rather narrow goals. Admiral Rickover, for instance, had little interest in humanities education; he wanted the high schools to teach more science, so that the nation could produce more scientists and compete successfully in the Cold War. Similarly, the most influential of the New Social Studies advocates paid no attention to natural-science education — even though they advocated social-science education, on the ground that it taught the scientific method. The authority claimed by the reformers was either too small or impossibly large. None took the cultural authority to decide what skills and what areas of knowledge would be most important to the generation then passing through the schools. (The college professors did not do so either. Only at the end of the seventies — under pressure of falling enrollments — did the colleges begin to put some order into their liberal-arts programs. And then most of them followed the lead and the outlines of the program established by Dean Henry Rosovsky of Harvard University.)

The failure of the reformers to produce a curriculum had its counterpart in the realm of ideas; they — particularly the New Social Studies advocates — failed to defend their own goals on moral and philosophical grounds. After all, the notion that the schools should teach critical thinking and the scientific method implied a set of values that was not accepted by the progressive-fundamentalist center of the school establishment in the late fifties. Bertrand Russell once wrote that "the whole conception of truth is one which is difficult to reconcile with the usual ideals of citizenship," if only because "it is impossible to instill the scientific spirit into the young so long as any propositions are regarded as sacrosanct and not open to question."[121] Instead of fighting this battle, the New Social Studies advocates retreated into their role as technicians, experts in pedagogy. The upshot was that they could not defend themselves from the charges of moral relativism which eventually came from both left and right.

This retreat from the larger terrain of culture had another important consequence. To take the role of technician is necessarily to take a narrow view of what constitutes the training of a mind. In practice, many of the New Social Studies advocates relied on the authority of the social sciences. That authority served perfectly well within its own limits — that is, for the creation of high-school courses in anthropology, economics, and so on. But it proved a negative influence on many other areas of social-studies teaching. In the field of American history, for example, it tended to reinforce the tendency to ahistoricism and to the reduction of complex social phenomena to "problems" with solutions waiting somewhere for them. Taken seriously, the notion of "science" in the social sciences led to a mechanistic view of history and of human behavior in general. The "behavioral outcomes" sought by the New Social Studies reformers were at least intellectual rather than moral outcomes, but otherwise they were almost as simpleminded and reductive of child psychology as anything the progressives or fundamentalists proposed. With such defenders, critical thinking hardly needed enemies.

Progressive, fundamentalist, and mandarin — all three reform movements have contributed to the reductive view of history and the ahistoricism and the dullness that inhabit so many of the history texts. But there is another group of people who made a substantial contribution, and that is the professional educationists in the social studies. No matter what school-reform group has been in the ascendance, there have always been educationists to translate its general ideas into more specific and trivial ones and to make even the simplest issue incomprehensible. In the area of teaching, the educationists have in the past decade taken up "values clarification," "conflict resolution," "decision-making," and "cognitive moral development." One of them has managed the extraordinary feat of reinventing the Socratic dialogue while forgetting that though Socrates was a teacher, not all teachers are Socrates. At the same time, their rhetoric, never pithy, has in the hands of some of the most influential ballooned to pure hot air. Paul F. Brandwein, for instance, who formerly was an adjunct professor of education at the University of Pittsburgh and a director of the National Association for Research and Development in Education and is now the director of research for Harcourt Brace Jovanovich, has this to say about the modest art of teaching the social sciences:

> . . . the ways of the child and of the teacher and of the social scientist are not disparate and divergent, they are congruent and convergent [sic]. All begin with a legacy; all begin with a heritage; all begin with the concepts that are part of the cognitive and affective underpinning of their society. There is a continuity of concepts, through past, present, and future, and they affect all lives. All of us share the human condition in all its magnificence and pathos.[122]

The social-studies texts of the seventies bear the imprint of all the new educational movements. Many of them are, in fact, monuments — towers of Babel — to the art of the educationist. And the younger the children to be taught, the higher these towers are. The current Houghton Mifflin social-studies series for kindergarten through sixth grade lists a general editor, an editorial adviser, fifteen teacher-consultants, and six other consultants, among them a "values consultant." According to the introductory material that appears in the teachers' edition of each volume, the series contains "strategies . . . designed to increase empathy and decrease inclinations toward egocentrism, ethnocentrism, and stereotyping"; also "historical materials [that] become a basic ingredient in the crucible of learning, as children are motivated to introduce their own life experiences and get involved in 'doing history.'" This series is also said to improve children's "decision-making" and to contribute to their "making valid judgments about problems facing our global society."[123] While the Houghton Mifflin series promises to save the world, its Harcourt Brace competitor promises to save the child from moral darkness. Among the Harcourt Brace series' supplementary materials is *A Probe Into Values*; according to the teachers' edition, "This comprehensive values clarification program is packaged in a box and includes forty individual investigations presenting the child with a conflict in values within his own frame of reference."[124]

In defense of many of these textbooks, it must be said that the "values clarification" programs and "conceptual grids" are merely gimmicks, which have no more effect on children than the flaming swords used to have on the meat served in the Pump Room in Chicago. (When asked about the inevitable flaming swords, the manager of that restaurant was supposed to have said, "Well, the customers like it, and it doesn't hurt the meat too much.") For all the fancy talk, the new teaching strategies are hardly any more subtle and insidious than the old progressive-fundamentalist civics lectures. In one elementary series, the efforts to encourage valid decision-making seem to boil down to a lot of photographs of trash cans and other ecological aids; in another, the strategy to increase empathy consists of endless pictures of smiling, well-behaved children from various tropical climes. As for the "values clarification" programs for older children, these usually follow along the lines of the Watergate or Japanese-American-internment-camp problems suggested in the N.C.S.S. Yearbook. Since few teachers, and fewer children, could actually put themselves in the place of one of Nixon's aides in the winter of

1973, the valid decision of any child would be to give the pious answer expected of him. The behavioral outcome for the child would likely be a sudden rise in cynicism and doubt about the competence of the teacher — if not open snickering.

The question is why. Why is it that the school-reform movements have all been so intellectually reductive? Why in the profession most directly concerned with education should there be a level of anti-intellectualism and sheer mindlessness found in few other professions? And, finally, why is it that schoolteachers and parents make no protest against all the gimmickry and the bland Socialist-realism-style writing in the books that children have to read? In the nineteen-fifties, a number of intellectuals — Commager, Hofstadter, Barzun, and others — puzzled over these questions, and the second one in particular. The answers they gave revolved around the low pay and low status of the teaching profession and the success of the educationists in divorcing the teachers college from the rest of the university. These conditions still exist to some degree, but the answers seem inadequate. The federal government now spends much more on the schools than formerly; the division between the universities and the secondary-school establishment is not as clear as it was twenty years ago; and most of the school reformers in the sixties and seventies came from outside the ranks of the professional educationists. To look at the whole subject again in the nineteen-seventies is to suspect that the causes lie deeper still.

One possible reason for the intellectual reductiveness of pedagogical thinking lies in the very nature of the pursuit. The job of educationists and other pedagogues is not primarily to consider the merits of any particular subject but to determine what and how young people can best be taught. Because the human mind knows very little about itself, their profession is an art or a craft, not a science—and most obviously so when it comes to teaching normal secondary-school students. The trouble is not just that there are few great artists or craftsmen in any field but that definite answers are much more attractive than indefinite ones, even if the questions are indefinite. Teaching gimmicks are much like pop psychology: the educationists have as much incentive to invent them as the publishers have to use them in books. Then, because it is practically impossible to prove or disprove any educational proposition in a scientific fashion, almost any proposition has a chance of being taken seriously if it is accompanied by enough noise. All of this explains a good deal about the success of certain New Social Studies advocates and the relative obscurity of those who had sounder, though necessarily more indefinite, ideas about how to teach children intellectual skills.

The propensity of educationists and school reformers to want to mold the character, rather than the minds, of children, however, derives from another syndrome. The assumption of pedagogy is, after all, that children are different from adults. From this assumption it is possible to proceed to the conclusion that children (even high-school students) are *very* different from adults — weird, deformed creatures who require salvation rather than simply schooling in history or English. While the Puritans believed that children were naturally sinful and had to be educated to virtue, modern pedagogues tend to believe that children are mentally ill. (The latest word on this subject comes from Paul Brandwein. "Above all," he has written, "a teacher heals." And, "In the social sciences, if nowhere else, a consideration of the child's development and mental health, within the purview of the meanings of civilization, is paramount.")[125] Similarly, the study of teaching methods carries with it the assumption that children can and should be manipulated in certain ways. On this line of reasoning, it is possible to proceed to the proposition that the aim of teaching is to obtain as much control over children as possible. It is not necessary to proceed in this direction — any more than it is necessary to believe that children are mentally ill — but in practice many professional educationists and their critics have done so in varying degrees. Pedagogy, in sum, is not just a vague and confusing subject, it is dangerous to those who think about it for too long.

The professional deformation of pedagogues probably does not entirely explain the simplistic behaviorism of so much educational thinking. Within the school-reform movements, at least, there is a larger social phenomenon at work. Americans, not uniquely but characteristically, want their children to have better lives and to live in a better world than they did. This desire has moved a great many mountains; it is at least partially responsible for all the great achievements of American society, including all of those connected with schooling. Still, where education is concerned, that desire is double-edged. In the first place, Americans, unlike those who live in static, class-bound societies, take a more or less utilitarian view of schooling. Usefulness could hardly be a more proper criterion for education. But the danger is that it is defined so narrowly as to permit only those skills that can immediately be put to use — or, worse still, nothing more than grades and degrees. In the second place, Americans tend to expect far too much from schooling. Of the two phenomena, the second is by far the more complex in cause and in result. At least since the nineteenth century, Americans have believed in the power of education in general, and schooling in particular, to improve the lot of their children and to improve society. John Dewey was speaking not as an educationist but as a philosopher in the American tradition when he said that the great discovery of the twentieth century was the child. This belief in education and in the future is, however, politically ambiguous. It could signify a great openness to change and a willingness to promote reform, but it could also signify the reverse. To urge reform through education could be merely a piece of wishful thinking or could be a strategy for avoiding reform, and the social conflict it would entail, by putting it off into the future. To urge reform through the public-school system could be merely to displace responsibility from the adult institutions that could achieve it. And, in practice, Americans in this century have sometimes placed burdens on children which they themselves were unwilling to shoulder, and put far too great a weight of responsibility on the schools.

Consider the question of social mobility, or equality of opportunity, to begin with. In this century, it has been a very firmly held article of belief that the public-high-school system was egalitarian and was the way for people from lower economic groups to rise on the economic ladder. If such a statement means that there is some correlation between academic achievement and economic success, then it is clearly true. But if it means that academic success is the decisive factor — that it is always more important than, say, the color of one's skin or the economic standing of one's parents — then it is clearly false. The schools cannot create equality of opportunity all by themselves. That seems quite obvious, and yet that is what many have expected them to do. Racial integration provides a similar case in point. Since the Supreme Court decisions of the nineteen-fifties, the burden of fulfilling what seemed to be a national aspiration for racial integration has been placed more heavily on the schools than on adult institutions such as corporations, labor unions, or government programs. The strategy is self-defeating — assuming that it was meant to work — since any particular tactic, from busing to "affirmative action," must cause some hardship to some students, and it is easier to raise a sympathy vote on behalf of children than on behalf of adults. In practice, the racial integration of the schools has been so easily circumvented as to prove that the schools by themselves cannot integrate society. Social welfare is yet another example. The progressive educators of the early nineteen-hundreds asked the schools to assume responsibility for the health, vocation, "worthy home membership," and use of leisure of the next generation. They passed over academic achievement for these things — and understandably, since they saw the public-school system as the one public agency available to meet the pressing needs of the new immigrants. The progressives of the nineteen-sixties asked the schools to meet much the same set of needs for children in the urban ghettos — there still being no adequate alternative.

Schooling is not all of education, and yet it has often been saddled with the responsibility for all of it. "Concerned citizens" groups will, for example, go to absurd lengths to take the word "damn" out of literary anthologies and anatomical drawings out of biology books, when the word is heard on every street corner and when really pornographic pictures can be found on the magazine racks of the local drugstore. This may be wishful thinking or it may be pure hypocrisy, a variation on the theme of "let us be saved but not too soon" — that is, "let us be saved by the next generation."

Not only fundamentalists but progressives as well have a strong tendency to think that the schools should present the world, or the country, as an ideal construct. The censorship of schoolbooks is simply the negative face of the demand that the books portray the world as a utopia of the eternal present — a place without conflicts, without malice or stupidity, where Dick (black or white) comes home with a smiling Jane to a nice house in the suburbs. To the extent that young people actually believe them, these bland fictions, propagated for the purpose of creating good citizens, may actually achieve the opposite; they give young people no warning of the real dangers ahead, and later they may well make these young people feel that their own experience of conflict or suffering is unique in history and perhaps un-American. To the extent that children can see the contrast between these fictions and the world around them, this kind of instruction can only make them cynical. The textbooks' naïveté about child psychology is matched only by their lack of respect for history. Indeed, to insist that children do as we say, not as we do, is to assert that the past has no influence over the future and that today peels away from yesterday like a decal. Yet, since the Progressive era, those responsible for the majority of American-history texts have been paying mere lip service to the truism that one must know history in order to understand the present and the future. To teach history with the assumption that students have the psychology of laboratory pigeons is not only to close off the avenues for thinking about the future; it is to deprive American children of their birthright.

Notes and Bibliography

Notes

1. Wood, Gabriel, and Biller, *America* (1975), p. 3.
2. King and Anderson, *The United States*, sixth level, Houghton Mifflin Social Studies Program (1976), pp. 15–16.
3. Sellers et al., *As It Happened* (1975), p. 812.
4. Graff, *The Free and the Brave*, 2nd ed. (1972), p. 696; and Graff and Krout, *The Adventure*, 2nd ed. (1973), p. 784.
5. Wood, Gabriel, and Biller, *America* (1975), p. 812.
6. Fenton, gen. ed., *A New History of the United States*, grade eleven (1969), p. 170.
7. Brandwein et al., *The Social Sciences* (1975), introductions to all books.
8. Ver Steeg and Hofstadter, *A People* (1974), pp. 722–723.
9. *New York Times*, 2 January 1977.
10. Muzzey, *A History* (1936), p. 420.
11. Ver Steeg and Hofstadter, *A People* (1974), p. 448.
12. Kownslar and Frizzle, *Discovering American History* (1974), and Fenton, gen. ed., *The Americans: A History* (1975).
13. National Education Association, Teacher Rights Division, *Inquiry Report: Kanawha County, West Virginia: A Textbook Study in Cultural Conflict* (February 1975).
14. State of Florida, Department of Education, *Criteria for Institutional Materials Selection in the Elementary Schools* (1976), p. 9.
15. Nelson and Roberts, *The Censors and the Schools* (1963), pp. 129–131.
16. Ibid., pp. 31–33.
17. Ibid., p. 39.
18. See ibid., chap. 8, "Glowing and Throbbing History," pp. 134–150.
19. Ibid., p. 134.
20. Black, *The American Schoolbook* (1967), pp. 108–114.
21. Ibid., p. 123.

22. Holt, Rinehart & Winston, School Department, *Guidelines for the Development of Elementary and Secondary Instructional Materials: Treatment of Sex Roles* (1975), p. 3.
23. Houghton Mifflin Company, *Avoiding Stereotypes: Principles and Applications* (1975), p. 23.
24. The Macmillan Company, *Guidelines for Creating Positive Sexual and Racial Images in Educational Materials* (1975), p. 43.
25. Madison, *Book Publishing in America* (1966), pp. 124–125.
26. John P. Dessauer, Inc., compiler, *Annual Industry Sales Statistics:* 1977 (1978).
27. Livengood, *Americana* (1954), p. 53, excerpt from Jedidiah Morse, *Geography Made Easy* (New Haven, 1784).
28. Willard, *History of the United States* (1847).
29. Fell, *The Foundations* (1941), p. 20.
30. Hart, *School History of the United States*, rev. ed. (1928), p. 127.
31. Hart, *New American History* (1917), p. 342.
32. West, *American History and Government* (1913), p. 296.
33. Ibid., p. 706.
34. Vannest and Smith, *Socialized History* (1931), p. 16.
35. Muzzey, *A History* (1950), p. 257.
36. Muzzey, *An American History* (1911), p. 164.
37. Ibid., p. 618.
38. Ibid., p. 622.
39. Muzzey, *A History* (1936), p. 437.
40. Ibid., p. 35.
41. Muzzey, *An American History* (1911), p. 509.
42. Hofstadter, *The Age of Reform* (1955), pp. 139–140 and 143–144.
43. Muzzey, *An American History* (1911), p. 622.
44. Guitteau, *Our United States: A History* (1923), p. 514.
45. Barker, Dodd, and Commager, *Our Nation's Development* (1937), p. 627.
46. Vannest and Smith, *Socialized History* (1931), p. 49.
47. Rugg, *An Introduction to the Problems of American Culture*, in Rugg Social Sciences Course (1931), V, 590.
48. Muzzey, *A History* (1955), pp. 2–3.
49. Moon and Cline, *Story of Our Land and People* (1964), pp. 558–559; Moon, Cline, and MacGowan, *Story* (1955), pp. 498–499; Wilder, Ludlum, and Brown, *This Is America's Story* (1948), pp. 492–495 and 504–508; and Hartman, *America: Land of Freedom* (1952), pp. 516–519.
50. Todd and Curti, *America's History* (1950), pp. 442–445; West and West, *The Story of Our Country* (1948), p. 384; Hamm, *From Colony to World Power* (1950), pp. 449–450.

51. Muzzey, *A History* (1950), p. 3.
52. See Wirth, *United States History* (1954); Moon, *Story of Our Land and People*, rev. ed. (1948); and Harlow, *Story of America* (1943), for representative versions of Reconstruction.
53. Caughey, Franklin, and May, *Land of the Free* (1966), was a pioneer in this respect.
54. Grob and Billias, eds., *Interpretations of American History*, 2nd ed. (1972), II, 25–39.
55. Goodrich, *A History* (1833), p. 37.
56. See Hart, *School History* (1918); and Hurlbert, *United States History* (1923); quote comes from Halleck, *History* (1923), p. 43.
57. Halleck, *History* (1923), p. 28.
58. Graff and Krout, *The Adventure* (1973), p. 16.
59. Jones, *O Strange New World* (1973), pp. 85–86.
60. Moon, Cline, and MacGowan, *Story* (1955), pp. 525–527; and Bourne and Benton, *A History* (1925), pp. 480 ff.
61. Educational Research Council of America, Social Science Staff, *American Adventure* (1975), I, A-89; and Leinwand, *The Pageant* (1975), p. 22.
62. Glazer and Moynihan, *Beyond the Melting Pot*, 2nd ed. (1970).
63. See Graff, *The Free and the Brave* (1972); Graff and Krout, *The Adventure* (1973); and Reich and Biller, *Building the American Nation*, new ed. (1971).
64. Racism and Sexism Resource Center for Educators, *Stereotypes* (1977), p. 75.
65. Halleck, *History* (1923); Hart, *School History* (1918); and Fish, *History of America* (1925).
66. West, *American History and Government* (1913), p. 703.
67. Beard and Beard, *History* (1923), pp. 379, 409.
68. Current, De Conde, and Dante, *United States History* (1974), p. 288 and pp. 303–304.
69. Wood, Gabriel, and Biller, *America* (1975), pp. 793–794.
70. Ibid., p. 794.
71. Reid, *An Adventure* (1969), pp. 34–36.
72. Casner and Gabriel, *The Story* (1955), p. 649.
73. Bragdon and McCutchen, *History* (1954), pp. 654, 667.
74. Moon and Cline, *Story of Our Land and People* (1964), p. 695.
75. Graff, *The Free and the Brave* (1967), p. 690.
76. Platt and Drummond, *Our Nation*, 2nd ed. (1967), p. 900.
77. Todd and Curti, *The Rise*, 3rd ed. (1972), II, 786.
78. Leinwand, *The Pageant* (1975), p. 646.
79. Wiltz, *The Search* (1973), p. 761.

80. Ver Steeg and Hofstadter, *A People* (1974), pp. 808–811.
81. Sellers et al., *As It Happened* (1975); Kownslar and Frizzle, *Discovering American History* (1974).
82. Wilder, Ludlum, and Brown, *This Is America's Story*, 4th ed. (1975), p. 708
83. Todd and Curti, *The Rise* (1972), p. 801; Wiltz, *The Search* (1973), p. 762.
84. Current, De Conde, and Dante, *United States History* (1974), p. 632.
85. Bragdon and McCutchen, *History* (1954), p. 277.
86. Ibid., p. 666.
87. Ibid.
88. Muzzey, *Our Country's History* (1957), p. 657.
89. Wiltz, *The Search* (1973), pp. 265–267.
90. Graff and Krout, *The Adventure* (1959), p. 672.
91. Kownslar and Frizzle, *Discovering* (1974), p. 715.
92. Ibid., p. 750.
93. Wilder, Ludlum, and Brown, *This Is America's Story* (1975).
94. Todd and Curti, *The Rise* (1972).
95. Wood, Gabriel, and Biller, *America* (1975), p. 635.
96. Muzzey, *A History* (1955), p. 506.
97. Todd and Curti, *The Rise* (1972), pp. 632–633.
98. Ibid., p. 417.
99. Current, De Conde, and Dante, *United States History* (1974), p. 601.
100. Wood, Gabriel, and Biller, *America* (1975), p. 635.
101. Fenton, gen. ed., *A New History of the United States*, grade eight (1975), p. 544.
102. Burns et al., *Episodes* (1973), pp. D95–D105.
103. Fenton, gen. ed., *The Americans: A History* (1970), pp. 462–463.
104. Hertzberg, *Historical Parallels* (1970).
105. Hofstadter, *Anti-Intellectualism* (1966), chap. 13, "The Road to Life Adjustment," pp. 323–358.
106. Dewey, *Democracy and Education* (1916), p. 88.
107. Committee on Concepts and Values, *A Guide to Content in the Social Studies* (1958).
108. Barzun, *The House of Intellect* (1959), pp. 120 ff.
109. Commager, *The Commonwealth of Learning* (1968), p. 12.
110. Bruner, *Toward a Theory of Instruction* (1967), pp. 35, 36.
111. Educational Research Council of America, Social Science Staff, *American Adventure* (1975), I, A-5.
112. Hertzberg, "The New Curriculum" (1973), pp. 1–5.
113. Massialas and Cox, *Inquiry in Social Studies* (1966), p. 5.
114. Weeden, Kenneth, "Teaching Decision Making in Secondary School Studies," in *Developing Decision Making Skills*, ed.

Dana G. Kurfman (Washington, D.C.: N.C.S.S., 1977), pp. 201–233.

115. Kownslar, ed., *Teaching American History* (1974), p. 11.
116. Fenton, "Moral Education" (1976).
117. Shaver, "A Critical View" (1977), p. 305.
118. Kozol, "The Search," *New York Times*, 2 February 1976.
119. Conlan and Dow, "Pro/Con Forum" (1975), pp. 388–396.
120. Cremin, *The Transformation of the Schools* (1961), pp. 253–257.
121. Russell, *Education and the Modern World* (1932), pp. 23, 105.
122. Brandwein, *Notes on Teaching* (1969), p. 7.
123. Anderson, gen. ed., *Windows* (1976), teacher's edition of each volume.
124. Brandwein et al., *The Social Sciences* (1975), teacher's edition of grade four text.
125. Brandwein, *Notes on Teaching* (1969), pp. 1, 11.

Bibliography

UNITED STATES HISTORY TEXTS: NINETEENTH CENTURY

Eggleston, Edward A. A *Household History of the United States and Its People for Young Americans*. New York: D. Appleton, 1889.

Goodrich, Charles A. A *History of the United States of America: From the Discovery of the Continent by Christopher Columbus to the Present Time*. Hartford: H. F. Sumner and Company, 1833. First edition, 1822.

——— *History of the United States of America: From the Discovery of the Continent by Christopher Columbus to the Present Time*. Revised by William H. Seavey. Boston: Brewer and Tileston, 1867.

Lee, Susan Pendleton. A *School History of the United States*. Richmond: B. F. Johnson, 1895.

Lossing, Benson J. A *Common-School History of the United States from the Earliest Period to the Present Time*. New York: Mason Brothers, 1865.

McMaster, John Bach. *A School History of the United States.* New York: American Book Company, 1897.

Montgomery, David Henry. *The Student's American History.* Boston: Ginn & Company, 1897.

Quackenbos, G. P. *Illustrated School History of the United States and Adjacent Parts of America from the Earliest Discoveries to the Present Time.* New York: D. Appleton, 1867.

Steele, Joel Dorman, and Esther Baker Steele. *A Brief History of the United States for Schools.* New York: A. S. Barnes and Company, 1871.

Willard, Emma (Hart). *History of the United States or, Republic of America.* New York: A. S. Barnes and Company, 1847.

UNITED STATES HISTORY TEXTS: 1900–1930

Ashley, Roscoe Lewis. *American History.* New York: Macmillan, new and revised, 1924. First edition, 1907.

Beard, Charles A., and William C. Bagley. *The History of the American People.* New York: Macmillan, revised 1923. First edition, 1918.

Beard, Charles, and Mary R. Beard. *History of the United States: A Study in American Civilization.* New York: Macmillan, 1923. First edition, 1921.

Bourne, Henry Eldridge, and Elbert Jay Benton. *A History of the United States.* New York: D. C. Heath, 1925. First edition, 1913.

Fish, Carl Russell. *History of America.* New York: American Book Company, 1925.

Guitteau, William Backus. *Our United States: A History.* New York: Silver Burdett, 1923. First edition, 1919.

Halleck, Reuben Post. *History of Our Country for Higher Grades.* New York: American Book Company, 1923.

Hart, Albert Bushnell. *New American History.* New York: American Book Company, 1917.

——— *School History of the United States.* New York: American Book Company, revised 1928. First edition, 1918.

Hurlbert, Archer Butler. *United States History.* Garden City: Doubleday, Page, 1923.

Shortridge, Wilson Porter. *The Development of the United States.* New York: Macmillan, 1929.

Tryon, Rolla M., and Charles R. Lingley. *The American People and Nation.* Boston: Ginn, 1927.

West, Willis Mason. *American History and Government.* Boston: Allyn & Bacon, 1913.

UNITED STATES HISTORY TEXTS: 1930–1950

Adams, James Truslow, and Charles Garrett Vannest. *The Record of America.* New York: Charles Scribner's Sons, 1935.

Barker, Eugene C., Henry Steele Commager, and Walter P. Webb. *The Building of Our Nation.* Evanston: Row, Peterson and Company, 1937.

Barker, Eugene C., William E. Dodd, and Henry Steele Commager. *Our Nation's Development.* Evanston: Row, Peterson, and Company, 1937. First edition, 1934.

Barker, Eugene C., Walter P. Webb, and William E. Dodd. *The Growth of a Nation.* Evanston: Row, Peterson and Company, 1934. First edition, 1928.

Canfield, Leon Hardy, and Howard B. Wilder. *The United States in the Making.* Boston: Houghton Mifflin, 1948.

Faulkner, Harold Underwood, and Tyler Kepner. *America: Its History and People.* New York: Harper Brothers, fifth edition, 1950. First edition, 1934.

Faulkner, Harold Underwood, Tyler Kepner, and Edward H. Merrill. *History of the American Way.* New York: Harper Brothers, 1950. First edition, 1941, under the title *The American Way of Life: A History.*

Freeland, George Earl. *America's Progress in Civilization.* Contributing editor, James Truslow Adams. New York: Charles Scribner's Sons, 1936.

Freeman, Melville. *The Story of Our Republic.* Edited by Eston V. Tubbs. Philadelphia: F. A. Davis, 1941.

Hamm, William Albert. *The American People.* Boston: D. C. Heath, 1942. First edition, 1938.

——— *From Colony to World Power: A History of the United States.* Boston: D. C. Heath, 1947, 1950. A reworking of *The American People.*

Harlow, Ralph. *Story of America.* New York: Henry Holt, 1943. First edition, 1937.

Latané, John Holladay. *The History of the American People.* Boston: Allyn & Bacon, 1930, 1932.

——— *History of the United States.* Boston: Allyn & Bacon, 1918, 1938.

Moon, Glenn W. *Story of Our Land and People.* New York: Henry Holt, revised edition, 1948. First edition, 1936.

Riegel, Robert Edgar, and Helen Haugh. *The United States of America: A History.* New York: Charles Scribner's Sons, 1947.

Rugg, Harold. *A History of American Civilization: Economic and Social.* Boston: Ginn, 1930. This is the third volume of the Rugg Social Science Course, Reading Books.

——— *An Introduction to the Problems of American Culture.* Boston: Ginn, 1931. This is the fifth volume of the Rugg Social Science Course, Reading Books.

Todd, Lewis Paul, and Merle Curti. *America's History.* New York: Harcourt Brace, 1950.

Tryon, Rolla M., Charles R. Lingley, and Frances Morehouse. *The American Nation Yesterday and Today.* Boston: Ginn, 1938. First edition, 1930.

Vannest, Charles Garrett, and Henry Lester Smith. *Socialized History of the United States.* New York: Charles Scribner's Sons, 1931, 1940, 1946.

West, Willis Mason, and Ruth West. *The American People: A New History for High Schools.* Boston: Ginn, 1934. First edition, 1928, by W. M. West.

——— *The Story of Our Country.* Boston: Allyn & Bacon, 1948.

UNITED STATES HISTORY TEXTS: 1950–1970

Augspurger, Everett, and Richard A. McLemore. *Our Nation's Story.* Chicago: Laidlaw Brothers, 1954.

Boller, Paul F., and E. Jean Tilford. *This Is Our Nation.* St. Louis: Webster Publishing Company, 1961.

Bragdon, Henry W., and Samuel P. McCutchen. *History of a Free People.* New York: Macmillan, 1954, 1961.

Bronz, Stephen H., W. Glenn Moon, and Don C. Cline. *The Challenge of America.* New York: Holt, Rinehart & Winston, 1968. A portion of this work was formerly copyrighted as *Story of Our Land and People,* 1957.

Caughey, John W., John Hope Franklin, and Ernest R. May. *Land of the Free: A History of the United States.* New York: Benziger Brothers, 1966.

Fenton, Edwin, general editor. *A New History of the United States: An Inquiry Approach.* By Irving Bartlett, Edwin Fenton, David Fowler, and Seymour Mandelbaum. New York: Holt, Rinehart & Winston, 1969. This is the text for grade eleven in the Carnegie-Mellon Social Studies Curriculum Series for grades nine through twelve, edited by Edwin Fenton. First published in 1966.

Gavian, Ruth Wood, and William A. Hamm. *United States History.* Boston: D. C. Heath, 1960.

Graff, Henry F. *The Free and the Brave: The Story of the American People.* Chicago: Rand McNally, 1967.

——— and John A. Krout. *The Adventure of the American People.* New York: Rand McNally, 1959, 1960, 1965.

Harlow, Ralph Volney, and Ruth Elizabeth Miller. *Story of America*. New York: Henry Holt, revised edition, 1953.

Hartman, Gertrude. *America: Land of Freedom*. Boston: D. C. Heath, 1952, second edition 1955. First edition, 1946.

Kownslar, Allan O., and Donald B. Frizzle. *Discovering American History*. New York: Holt, Rinehart & Winston, 1967.

Moon, Glenn W., and Don C. Cline. *Story of Our Land and People*. New York: Holt, Rinehart and Winston, 1964.

Moon, Glenn W., Don C. Cline, and John H. MacGowan. *Story of Our Land and People*. New York: Henry Holt, 1955.

Platt, Nathaniel, and Muriel Jean Drummond. *Our Nation from Its Creation: A Great Experiment*. Englewood Cliffs: Prentice-Hall, 1967. First edition, 1966.

Reich, Jerome R., and Edward L. Biller. *Building the American Nation*. New York: Harcourt, Brace and World, 1968.

Schwartz, Melvin, and John O'Connor. *Exploring American History*. New York: The Globe Book Company, fourth edition, 1968. First edition, 1963.

Todd, Lewis Paul, and Merle Curti. *The Rise of the American Nation*. New York: Harcourt, Brace and World, 1961, 1966, 1969. First edition, 1950.

Wilder, Howard B., Robert P. Ludlum, and Harriet McCune Brown. *This Is America's Story*. Boston: Houghton Mifflin, 1948, 1958, 1963, 1968.

Wirth, Fremont P. *United States History*. New York: American Book Company, 1948, 1954.

UNITED STATES HISTORY TEXTS: 1970S

Branson, Margaret Stimmann. *Land of Challenge*. Consultants, Irwin Unger and H. Mark Johnson. Lexington, Mass.: Ginn, 1975.

Burns, Robert E., et al. *Episodes in American History: An Inquiry Approach*. 4 vols. Boston: Ginn, 1973.

Chapin, June R., Raymond J. McHugh, and Richard E. Gross. *Quest for Liberty: Investigating United States History*. Palo Alto: Field Educational Publications, 1971.

Current, Richard N., Alexander De Conde, and Harris L. Dante. *United States History: Search for Freedom*. Glenview: Scott, Foresman, 1974.

Educational Research Council of America, Social Science Staff. *The American Adventure*. Volume I. Boston: Allyn & Bacon, 1975.

Fenton, Edwin, general editor. *The Americans: A History of the United States*. By the Social Studies Curriculum Center Staff,

Carnegie-Mellon University, for grade eight. Published by American Heritage Publishing Company, distributed by Holt, Rinehart & Winston, New York, 1970, 1975.

——— *A New History of the United States: An Inquiry Approach.* By Irwin Bartlett, Edwin Fenton, David Fowler, and Seymour Mandelbaum. New York: Holt, Rinehart & Winston, 1975. In the Holt Social Studies Curriculum for grades nine through twelve. First published in 1966.

Fielder, William R., general editor. *Inquiring about American History: Studies in History and Political Science.* Major contributor, Allan O. Kownslar. New York: Holt, Rinehart & Winston, 1972, 1975. This is the integrated teacher's manual for level five of the Holt Data Bank System, William R. Fielder, general editor for grades kindergarten through six.

Graff, Henry F. *The Free and the Brave: The Story of the American People.* Chicago: Rand McNally, 1972. First edition, 1967.

——— and John A. Krout. *The Adventure of the American People.* Chicago: Rand McNally, second edition, revised printing, 1973.

King, David C., and Charlotte C. Anderson. *The United States.* Boston: Houghton Mifflin, 1976. This is the sixth-level text in *Windows on Our World,* the Houghton Mifflin Social Studies Program; Lee F. Anderson, general editor.

Kownslar, Allan O., and Donald B. Frizzle. *Discovering American History.* New York: Holt, Rinehart & Winston, 1974. First edition, 1967.

Leinwand, Gerald. *The Pageant of American History.* Boston: Allyn & Bacon, 1975.

Reich, Jerome R., and Edward L. Biller. *Building the American Nation.* New York: Harcourt Brace Jovanovich, new edition, 1971. First edition, 1968.

Reich, Jerome R., Arvarh E. Strickland, and Edward L. Biller. *Building the United States.* New York: Harcourt Brace Jovanovich, 1971.

Sandler, Martin W., Edwin C. Rozwenc, and Edward C. Martin. *The People Make a Nation.* Boston: Allyn & Bacon, 1975.

Sellers, Charles G., et al. *As It Happened: A History of the United States.* New York: McGraw-Hill, 1975.

Todd, Lewis Paul, and Merle Curti. *The Rise of the American Nation.* Volumes I and II. New York: Harcourt Brace Jovanovich, third edition, 1972.

Unger, Irwin, and H. Mark Johnson. *Land of Progress.* Lexington, Mass.: Ginn, 1975.

Ver Steeg, Clarence L., and Richard Hofstadter. *A People and a Nation.* New York: Harper & Row, 1971. Edition used was printed in 1974.

Weinstein, Allen, and R. Jackson Wilson. *Freedom and Crisis: An American History*. New York: Random House, 1974.
Wilder, Howard B., Robert P. Ludlum, and Harriet McCune Brown. *This Is America's Story*. Boston: Houghton Mifflin, 1970; fourth edition, 1975.
Wiltz, John Edward. *The Search for Identity: Modern American History*. Philadelphia: J. B. Lippincott, 1973.
Wood, Leonard C., Ralph H. Gabriel, and Edward L. Biller. *America: Its People and Values*. New York: Harcourt Brace Jovanovich, 1971, 1975.

UNITED STATES SOCIAL-STUDIES TEXTS: 1970S

Anderson, Lee F., general editor. *Windows on Our World*. Boston: Houghton Mifflin, 1976. This is the Houghton Mifflin Social Studies Program for seven levels.
Brandwein, Paul Franz, et al. *The Social Sciences: Concepts and Values*. 6 vols., seven levels, kindergarten through grade six. New York: Harcourt Brace Jovanovich, 1975. First edition, 1957.
Dimond, Stanley E., and Elmer F. Pflieger. *Our American Government*. Philadelphia: J. B. Lippincott, 1973. First edition, 1957.
Dunwiddie, William E. *Problems of Democracy: Political, Social, Economic*. Lexington, Mass.: Ginn, new edition, 1974. First edition, 1962.
Fenton, Edwin, Anthony N. Penna, and Mindella Schultz. *Comparative Political Systems: An Inquiry Approach*. New York: Holt, Rinehart & Winston, second edition, 1973. This is the text for grade nine in the Holt Social Studies Curriculum for grades nine through twelve, Edwin Fenton, general editor. First published in 1966.
Hartley, William Harrison, and William S. Vincent. *American Civics*. New York: Harcourt Brace Jovanovich, 1974. First edition, 1967.
Loewen, James W., and Charles Sallis, editors. *Mississippi: Conflict and Change*. New York: Pantheon Books, Random House, 1974.
Magruder, Frank Abbott. *American Government*. Revised by William A. McClenaghan. Boston: Allyn & Bacon, 58th edition, 1975. First edition, 1917. Also known as *Magruder's American Government*.
Mehlinger, Howard D., and John J. Patrick. *American Political Behavior*. Lexington, Mass.: Ginn, 1974. First edition, 1972.
Schick, Allen, and Adrienne Pfister. *American Government: Continuity and Change*. Boston: Houghton Mifflin, 1972.

Shaver, James P., and A. Guy Larkins. *Decision-Making in a Democracy*. Howard D. Mehlinger, editorial advisor. Boston: Houghton Mifflin, 1973.
Todd, Lewis Paul, and Merle Curti. *The Rise of the American Nation*. Volume II, *1865 to the Present*. New York: Harcourt Brace Jovanovich, third edition, 1972.
Wade, Richard C., Howard B. Wilder, and Louise C. Wade. *A History of the United States*. Boston: Houghton Mifflin, 1972. First edition, 1966.
Woll, Peter, and Robert H. Binstock. *America's Political System: People, Government, Policies*. New York: Random House, 1972.

MABEL B. CASNER AND RALPH HENRY GABRIEL TEXTS

Casner, Mabel B., and Ralph Henry Gabriel. *Exploring American History*. New York: Harcourt, Brace, 1931, 1935.
——— *The Rise of American Democracy*. New York: Harcourt, Brace, 1938.
——— *The Story of American Democracy*. New York: Harcourt, Brace, 1942, 1950, 1955.

DAVID SAVILLE MUZZEY TEXTS

Muzzey, David Saville. *An American History*. Boston: Ginn, 1911, 1925.
——— *A History of Our Country: A Textbook for High School Students*. Boston: Ginn, 1936, 1948, 1950, 1955.
——— *Our Country's History*. Boston: Ginn, 1957, 1961.
——— and Arthur S. Link. *Our American Republic*. Boston: Ginn, 1963, 1966.

SECONDARY SOURCES

American Historical Association, Committee of Seven. *The Study of History in Schools*. Report to the American Historical Association. New York: Macmillan, 1899.
American Textbook Publishers Institute. *Textbooks in Education: A Report from the American Textbook Publishers Institute to Its Membership, Its Friends, and Any Others Whose Interest in the Development of the Educational System in the United States Goes beyond a Mere Passing Fancy*. New York, 1949.

Anyon, Jean. "Ideology and U.S. History Texts: A Study of Bias." Paper presented to the 1976 annual meeting of the N.C.S.S.

Armbruster, Frank E. "The More We Spend, the Less Children Learn," *The New York Times Magazine* (August 28, 1977), pp. 9–11 ff.

The Asia Society, New York City. *Asia in American Textbooks: An Evaluation Based on a Study Conducted by the Asia Society with Support from the Ford Foundation*, 1976.

Barzun, Jacques. *The House of Intellect*. New York: Harper Brothers, 1959.

Black, Hillel. *The American Schoolbook*. New York: William Morrow, 1967.

Bolster, Arthur S., Jr. "History, Historians, and the Secondary School Curriculum." In James P. Shaver and Harold Berlek, editors, *Democracy, Pluralism and the Social Studies*, pp. 212–235. Boston: Houghton Mifflin, 1968.

Boorstin, Daniel Joseph. *The Americans: The Colonial Experience.* New York: Vintage Books, 1958.

——— *The Americans: The National Experience*. New York: Vintage Books, 1965.

Brandwein, Paul Franz. *Elements in a Strategy for Teaching Science in the Elementary School*. New York: Harcourt, Brace and World, reprint, n.d. Originally published by Harvard University Press, 1962.

——— *Notes on Teaching the Social Sciences: Concepts and Values*. New York: Harcourt, Brace and World, 1969.

——— "The Textbook: A Base for Instructed Learning." An address at the University of Bologna, April 1974.

Bruner, Jerome Seymour. *Toward a Theory of Instruction*. Cambridge: Belknap Press of Harvard University Press, 1967.

Butts, Freeman R., and Lawrence A. Cremin. *A History of Education in American Culture*. New York: Holt, Rinehart & Winston, 1953.

Carpenter, Charles. *History of American Schoolbooks*. Philadelphia: University of Pennsylvania Press, 1963.

Commager, Henry Steele. *The American Mind: An Interpretation of American Thought and Character since the 1880's*. New Haven: Yale University Press, 1950.

——— *The Commonwealth of Learning*. New York: Harper & Row, 1968.

Conlan, John B., and Peter B. Dow. "Pro/Con Forum: The MACOS Controversy: The Push for a Uniform National Curriculum [and] MACOS Revisited: A Commentary on the Most Frequently Asked About Questions about 'Man: A Course of Study,'" *Social Education* 39 (October 1975): 388–396.

Counts, George S. *Dare the School Build a New Social Order?* New York: The John Day Company, 1932.

Cremin, Lawrence A. *Public Education.* New York: Basic Books, 1976.

——— *Traditions of American Education.* New York: Basic Books, 1977.

——— *The Transformation of the Schools: Progressivism in American Education.* New York: Alfred A. Knopf, 1961.

Dewey, John. *Democracy and Education: An Introduction to the Philosophy of Education.* New York: Macmillan, 1916.

Elson, Ruth Miller. *Guardians of Tradition: American Schoolbooks in the Nineteenth Century.* Lincoln: University of Nebraska Press, 1964.

Fell, Sister Marie Léonore. *The Foundations of Nativism in American Textbooks, 1783–1860.* Washington, D.C.: The Catholic University of America Press, 1941.

Fenton, Edwin. *Developing a New Curriculum: A Rationale for the Holt Social Studies Curriculum.* New York: Holt, Rinehart & Winston, 1967.

——— "Moral Education: The Research Findings," *Social Education* 40 (April 1976): 188–193.

——— *The New Social Studies.* New York: Holt, Rinehart & Winston, 1967.

——— "A Response to Jack R. Fraenkel: An Exchange of Views between Fenton and Jack R. Fraenkel, the Cognitive-Developmental Approach to Moral Education," *Social Education* 41 (January 1977): 56–60.

——— *Teaching the New Social Studies in Secondary Schools: An Inductive Approach.* New York: Holt, Rinehart & Winston, 1966.

———, John M. Good, and Mitchell P. Lichtenberg. *A High School Social Studies Curriculum for Able Students: An Audio-Visual Component to a High School Studies Curriculum for Able Students.* Final report, Social Studies Curriculum Development Center, Carnegie-Mellon University. Washington, D.C.: U.S. Department of Health, Education and Welfare, Office of Education, Bureau of Research, April 1969.

Fischer, David Hackett. *Historians' Fallacies: Toward a Logic of Historical Thought.* New York: Harper & Row, 1970.

Florida Department of Education. *Criteria for Instructional Materials Selection in the Elementary Schools.* 1976.

Fraenkel, Jack R. "The Kohlberg Bandwagon: Some Reservations," *Social Education* 40 (April 1976): 216–222.

Fraser, Dorothy McClure, editor. *Social Studies Curriculum Development: Problems and Prospects.* National Council for the Social Studies, 39th Yearbook. Washington, D.C.: N.C.S.S., 1969.

Glazer, Nathan, and Daniel Patrick Moynihan. *Beyond the Melting Pot*. Cambridge: M.I.T. Press, second edition, 1970.

Griswold, William J. *The Image of the Middle East in Secondary School Textbooks*. New York: Middle East Studies Association of North America, 1975.

Grob, Gerald N., and George A. Billias, editors. *Interpretations of American History*. Volume II: *Since 1865*. New York: Macmillan, second edition, 1972.

Gross, Richard E. "The Status of the Social Sciences in the Public Schools of the United States: Facts and Impressions of a National Survey," *Social Education* 41 (March 1977): 194–200 ff.

Gwynn, J. Minor. *Curriculum Principles and Social Trends*. New York: Macmillan, 1960.

Handlin, Oscar. *The Americans: A New History of the People of the United States*. Boston: Atlantic–Little, Brown, 1963.

Hering, William M., Jr. "The Inquiry Method." In *Encyclopedia of Education*. New York: Macmillan and The Free Press, 1952.

Hertzberg, Hazel W. *Historical Parallels for the Sixties and Seventies: Primary Sources and Core Curriculum Revisited*. Publication No. 135, Social Science Consortium Inc., Boulder, Colorado, 1971.

——— "The New Curriculum Movement in the Social Studies: Uses of the Past and Implications for the Future," *Social Science Education Consortium Newsletter* 15 (April 1973): 1–5.

Hinckley, Rachel Francelia. "American Culture as Reflected in Mathematical Schoolbooks." Ph.D. dissertation, Teachers College of Columbia University, 1950.

Hofstadter, Richard. *The Age of Reform: From Bryan to F.D.R.* New York: Vintage Books, 1955.

——— *Anti-Intellectualism in American Life*. New York: Vintage Books, 1962.

Holt, Rinehart & Winston, School Department. *Guidelines for the Development of Elementary and Secondary Instructional Materials: Treatment of Sex Roles*. New York, 1975.

Houghton Mifflin Company. *Avoiding Stereotypes: Principles and Applications*. Boston, 1975.

Jarolimek, John. "Trends." In *Encyclopedia of Education*. New York: Macmillan and The Free Press, 1952.

Jencks, Christopher, et al. *Inequality: A Reassessment of the Effect of Family and Schooling in America*. New York: Harper Colophon Books, 1973.

Johnson, Clifton. *Old-Time Schools and Schoolbooks*. New York: Macmillan, reprinted 1917. First edition, 1904.

Johnson, Henry. *Teaching of History in Elementary and Secondary Schools*. New York: Macmillan, revised edition, 1940.

Jones, Howard Mumford. *The Age of Energy: Varieties of American Experience, 1865–1915*. New York: Viking Compass Books, 1973.

——— *O Strange New World: American Culture: The Formative Years*. New York: Viking Compass Books, fifth printing, 1973.

Kane, Michael B. *Minorities in Textbooks: A Study of Their Treatment in Social Studies Texts*. New York: Quadrangle Books, 1970.

Kirkendall, Richard S. "More History, Better History," *Social Education* 40 (October 1976): 446–451.

Kownslar, Allan O., editor. *Teaching American History: The Quest for Relevancy*. National Council for the Social Studies, 44th Yearbook. Washington, D.C.: N.C.S.S., 1974.

Kozol, Jonathan. "The Search for an Adjective That Will Cure Discrimination," *New York Times*, February 2, 1976.

Kurfman, Dana G., editor. *Developing Decision Making Skills*. National Council for the Social Studies, 47th Yearbook. Washington, D.C.: N.C.S.S., 1977.

Livengood, William Winfred. *Americana: As Taught to the Tune of a Hickory Stick*. New York: Women's National Book Association, 1954.

——— "Our Heritage." Address delivered to the American Book Company, Sinton Hotel, Cincinnati, Ohio, January 4, 1947.

——— *Our Textbooks Yesterday and Today*. Norwood, Mass.: Plimpton Press, 1953.

The Macmillan Company. *Guidelines for Creating Positive Sexual and Racial Images in Educational Materials*. New York, 1975.

Madison, Charles A. *Book Publishing in America*. New York: McGraw-Hill, 1966.

Makielski, Stanislaw J. *Beleaguered Minorities: Cultural Politics in America*. San Francisco: W. H. Freeman, 1973.

Massialas, Byron G., and C. Benjamin Cox. *Inquiry in Social Studies*. New York: McGraw-Hill, 1966.

Massialas, Byron G., and Andreas M. Kazamias, editors. *Crucial Issues in the Teaching of Social Studies: A Book of Readings*. Englewood Cliffs: Prentice-Hall, 1964.

McGraw-Hill. "McGraw-Hill Guidelines for Equal Treatment of the Sexes," *School Library Journal* 21 (January 1975): 23–27.

Morrissett, Irving. "Conceptual Approaches." In *Encyclopedia of Education*. New York: Macmillan and The Free Press, 1952.

National Council for the Social Sciences, Committee on Concepts and Values. *A Guide to Content in the Social Studies*. Washington, D.C.: N.C.S.S., 1958.

National Education Association, Committee of Ten on Secondary School Studies. *Report of the Committee on Secondary School Studies.* Washington, D.C.: U.S. Government Printing Office, 1893.

———, Commission on the Reorganization of Secondary Education. *Cardinal Principles of Secondary Education.* United States Office of Education Bulletin No. 35. Washington, D.C.: U.S. Government Printing Office, 1918.

——— Educational Policies Commission. *The Purposes of Education in American Democracy.* Washington, D.C.: U.S. Government Printing Office, 1938.

———, Teacher Rights Division. *Inquiry Report: Kanawha County, West Virginia: A Textbook Study in Cultural Conflict.* February 1975.

Nelkin, Dorothy. "The Science-Textbook Controversies," *Scientific American* 234 (April 1976): 33–39.

Nelson, Jack, and Gene Roberts, Jr. *The Censors and the Schools.* Boston: Little, Brown, 1963.

Nietz, John A. *Old Textbooks: Spelling, Grammar, Reading, Arithmetic, Geography, American History, Civil Government, Physiology, Penmanship, Art, Music, as Taught in the Common Schools from Early Colonial Days to 1900.* Pittsburgh: University of Pittsburgh Press, 1961.

Oliver, Donald W. "The Selection of Content in the Social Studies." In James P. Shaver and Harold Berlak, editors, *Democracy, Pluralism and the Social Studies,* pp. 17–42. Boston: Houghton Mifflin, 1968.

Patrick, John J. *Political Socialization of American Youth: Implications for Secondary School Studies, a Review of Research.* N.C.S.S. Research Bulletin No. 3. Washington, D.C.: N.C.S.S., 1967.

Pierce, Bessie Louise. *Civic Attitudes in American School Textbooks.* Chicago: University of Chicago Press, 1930.

Racism and Sexism Resource Center for Educators. *Stereotypes, Distortions and Omissions in U.S. History Textbooks: A Content Analysis Instrument for Detecting Racism and Sexism, Supplemental Information on Asian American, Black, Chicano, Native American, Puerto Rican, and Women's History.* New York: Council on Interracial Books for Children, 1977.

Rafferty, Max Lewis. *What Are They Doing to Your Children?* New York: New American Library, 1964.

Random House, Education Division, Guidelines Committee. *Guidelines for Multiethnic/Nonsexist Survey.* New York: 1975.

Ravitch, Diane. "Revisionists Revised: Studies in the Historiography of American Education," *Proceedings of the National Academy of Education* 4 (1977): 1–84.

Reid, James M. *An Adventure in Textbooks 1924–1960*. New York: R. R. Bowker, 1969.

Russell, Bertrand. *Education and the Modern World*. New York: W. W. Norton, 1932.

Shaver, James P. "A Critical View of the Social Studies Profession," N.C.S.S. presidential address, *Social Education* 41 (April 1977): 300–307.

——— "Reflective Thinking: Values and Social Studies Textbooks," *School Review* 73 (Autumn 1965): 226–257.

Shaver, James P., O. L. Davis, Jr., and Suzanne W. Helburn. "The Status of Social Studies Education: Impressions from Three NSF Studies," *Social Education* 43 (February 1979): 150–153.

Silberman, Charles E. *Crisis in the Classroom: The Remaking of American Education*. New York: Random House, 1970.

Thompson, Frank Victor. *Schooling of the Immigrant*. New York: Harper and Brothers, 1920.

Thursfield, Richard Emmons. *The Study and Teaching of American History*. National Council for the Social Studies, 17th Yearbook, 1946. Washington, D.C.: N.C.S.S., 1947.

Ubbelohde, Carl, and Jack R. Fraenkel, editors. *Values of the American Heritage: Challenge, Case Studies and Teaching Strategies*. National Council for the Social Studies, 45th Yearbook, 1975. Washington, D.C.: N.C.S.S., 1976.

U.S. House of Representatives, Committee on Education and Labor. *Books for Schools and the Treatment of Minorities*. Hearings before the Ad Hoc Subcommittee on De Facto School Segregation. 89th Congress, August-September, 1966.

Walworth, Arthur. *School Histories at War: A Study of the Treatment of Our Wars in the Secondary School History Books of the United States and Those of Its Former Enemies*. Cambridge: Harvard University Press, 1938.

Weinstein, Gerald, and Mario D. Fantani, editors. *Toward Humanistic Education: A Curriculum of Affect*. A Ford Foundation report. New York: Praeger, 1970.

Williams, T. Harry, Richard N. Current, and Frank Freidel. *A History of the United States to 1876*. New York: Alfred A. Knopf, 1959.

Woodward, Comer Vann. *Reunion and Reaction: The Compromise of 1877 and the End of Reconstruction*. New York: Doubleday Anchor Books, second revised edition, 1956. First edition, 1951.

Zimet, Sara Goodman. *What Children Read in Schools: Critical Analysis of Primary Reading Textbooks*. New York: Grune and Stratton, 1972.